WILLIAMS-SONOMA

Food & Wine Pairing

GENERAL EDITOR
Chuck Williams

RECIPES
Joyce Goldstein

WINE NOTES
Evan Goldstein

PHOTOGRAPHY
Richard Eskite

TIME
LIFE
BOOKS

TIME-LIFE BOOKS
Time-Life Books is a division of Time Life Inc.
Time-Life is a trademark of Time Warner Inc. U.S.A.

TIME-LIFE CUSTOM PUBLISHING
Vice President and Publisher: Terry Newell
Vice President of Sales and Marketing: Neil Levin
Director of Financial Operations: J. Brian Birky
Director of Acquisitions: Jennifer L. Pearce

WILLIAMS-SONOMA
Founder and Vice-Chairman: Chuck Williams
Associate Book Buyer: Cecilia Michaelis

WELDON OWEN INC.
President: John Owen
Vice President and Publisher: Wendely Harvey
Chief Operating Officer: Larry Partington
Vice President International Sales: Stuart Laurence
Series Editor: Val Cipollone
Managing Editor: Jamie Purviance
Consulting Editor: Norman Kolpas
Copy Editor: Sharon Silva
Design: Kari Perin, Perin+Perin
Production Director: Stephanie Sherman
Production Manager: Christine DePedro
Production Editor: Sarah Lemas
Food Stylist: Pouké
Prop Stylist: Laura Ferguson
Photo Production Coordinator: Juliann Harvey
Photo Assistant: Kevin Hossler
Food Styling Assistant: Jeff Tucker
Glossary Illustrations: Alice Harth

A NOTE ON WEIGHTS AND MEASURES
All recipes include customary U.S. and metric
measurements. Metric conversions are based on a
standard developed for these books and have been
rounded off. Actual weights may vary.

The Williams-Sonoma Lifestyles Series
conceived and produced by Weldon Owen Inc.
814 Montgomery Street, San Francisco, CA 94133

In collaboration with Williams-Sonoma
3250 Van Ness Avenue, San Francisco, CA 94109

Separations by Colourscan Overseas Co. Pte. Ltd.
Printed in Singapore by Tien Wah Press (Pte.) Ltd.

A WELDON OWEN PRODUCTION
Copyright © 1999 Weldon Owen Inc.
All rights reserved, including the right of repro-
duction in whole or in part in any form.

First printed in 1999
10 9 8 7 6 5 4 3 2 1

Library of Congress
Cataloging-in-Publication Data

Goldstein, Joyce Esersky.
    Food & wine pairing / general editor, Chuck
Williams; recipes, Joyce Goldstein; wine notes, Evan
Goldstein; photography, Richard Eskite.
        p. cm. — (Williams-Sonoma lifestyles)
    Includes index.
    ISBN 0-7370-2024-5
    1. Cookery. 2. Wine and wine making.
I. Goldstein, Evan. II. Williams, Chuck. III. Title.
IV. Food and wine pairing. V. Series.
TX714.G6485 1999
641.5—dc21   99-10022
                                          CIP

A NOTE ON NUTRITIONAL ANALYSIS
Each recipe is analyzed for significant nutrients per
serving. Not included in the analysis are ingredients
that are optional or added to taste, or are suggested
as an alternative or substitution either in the recipe
or in the recipe introduction or accompanying tip.
In recipes that yield a range of servings, the analysis
is for the middle of that range.

Contents

Welcome

For anyone who truly loves to dine rather than merely to eat, the words *wine* and *food* are inseparable. A thoughtfully selected glass of wine enhances the appreciation of the food with which it is paired. And when food is specially prepared to complement a fine wine, the wine shines at its brightest.

That is why I am so enthusiastic about this volume in the *Lifestyles* series and about the two people whose combined talents have created it. Joyce Goldstein, a chef whom I am happy to count among my friends, has developed inspired recipes that have affinities with several styles of wine. And her son, master sommelier Evan Goldstein, has made his expert recommendations of the specific types of wines that will taste best with the food.

In the introductory pages that follow, Evan Goldstein's philosophy behind such pairings is explained, along with advice on how to serve and store wines and suggestions for complete menus you can compose from the book's recipes. A concise glossary of wine terminology concludes this volume.

All these features share a simple goal: to eliminate the mystique that too often burdens this subject, and to maximize the pleasure you gain from serving wine and food together.

Chuck Williams

Pairing Wine & Food

The type of grapes used to make a particular wine most significantly affects its basic characteristics (top). Pickles, hot mustard, sweet chutney, artichokes, and chiles (clockwise from top left) are among the foods that tend to be difficult to pair with nearly all wines. The pairing of lobster and Chardonnay (far right) ranks high among the many classic food-and-wine combinations.

Fundamentals

By understanding six basic characteristics of food and wine explained here—sweetness, saltiness, acidity, bitterness, oak, and alcohol—you can make a more informed decision about what wine to pour with a specific food or, conversely, what food to cook when you want to highlight a particular wine. These six characteristics, in turn, form the foundation for the wine tips offered as part of the introductory notes that accompany every recipe in this book.

Each wine tip begins by explaining the core pairing issues unique to the dish. Two recommendations follow, one labeled "Dependable" and the other "Daring." Dependable wines are safe matches, the kind that a trustworthy sommelier might suggest. Daring recommendations, on the other hand, tend to be more imaginative and unusual, and are likely to please you in surprising ways. For more options to serve with any given recipe, refer to the chart on pages 10–13 and choose any of the wines listed under the category printed at the bottom of the recipe's page.

Sweetness

Some dry wines made from very ripe grapes give the illusion of being sweet, and go well with savory foods that are also slightly sweet. Off-dry wines with a trace of sweetness help soften the impact of spicy-hot dishes. Very sweet dessert wines should be carefully matched to foods that are equally sweet or slightly less so, or the wine will taste sour by comparison. Slightly sweet wines sometimes also contrast nicely with salty foods.

Saltiness

Table wines are not salty, but they can affect our perception of the salt present in foods. To counterbalance saltiness, try serving a sparkling or white wine that has good acidity, a quality that makes our mouths water and refreshes our sense of taste. Conversely, wines that are markedly bitter or high in alcohol can make salty foods taste even saltier.

Acidity

Wines high in acidity, or tartness, have the wonderful effect
of amplifying some of the subtle
flavors of food. High acidity also
provides a nice palate-cleansing
contrast to rich or oily foods.
When tart ingredients such as
vinegar or lemon juice are used
in recipes, acidic wines generally
make the best accompaniments.

Bitterness

The bitter factor in a wine's taste
comes from substances known as
tannins, which are present both in
grape skins and in the oak barrels
that are used for aging many
wines. Wines high in tannin go
best with dishes featuring naturally bitter ingredients or with
foods that acquire an edge of
bitterness through such cooking
methods as grilling or blackening.
These wines also counterbalance
the richness of foods high in fat,
such as cheese.

Oak

For wines that spend a lot of
time in oak before bottling, the
wood itself contributes distinctive flavor and character. Some
wines gain a smoothness and
roundness from oak that many
people enjoy with foods of the
same character. Oak can also
contribute flavors often described
with terms like toast, caramel,
and vanilla, which match well
with similar flavors in foods.
Oak's natural tannins, of course,
can contribute bitterness as well.

Alcohol

The presence of alcohol has an
effect on a wine's body. The
higher the alcohol content, the
richer in body, or "weightier,"
a wine seems. Lighter-bodied
wines are appropriate with
lighter ingredients and heavier
wines are best suited to heavier
foods. Also, be aware that the
higher a wine's alcohol content,
the more it will amplify your perception of salt and
hot spices.

Finding the Right Style

To help guide you in pairing wine with food, the following pages list dozens of widely available types of wine produced around the world. These are grouped into four broad categories: Sparkling and Rosé Wines; White Wines; Red Wines; and Dessert Wines. They are further broken down into subcategories based on the styles in which the particular wines are made. When looking for a wine to substitute for one suggested for a recipe, simply locate the subcategory printed at the bottom of the recipe's page.

You will notice that many wines are included in more than one category. This reflects the simple fact that different vintners, regions, or countries may use the same type of grape(s), but create markedly different styles of wine. Most labels, however, indicate the style in which the wine was produced, and wineshop owners, as well as magazine and newspaper articles on wine, can provide you with further guidance.

SPARKLING AND ROSÉ WINES

Dry Sparkling Wines
Light wines with little or no oak and no sweetness.
Cava (Spain)
Champagne (France)
Prosecco (Italy)
Rosé Champagne (France)
Rosé sparkling wine (USA)
Sparkling wine (USA)
Other sparkling wines (Australia, South America, New Zealand)

Off-Dry Rosé Wines
Light wines with hints of color and sweetness.
Rosé d'Anjou (France)
White Zinfandel (USA)
Other off-dry rosé wines (Australia, France, Spain, USA)

Dry Rosé Wines
Rich wines with a blush of color, moderate to high levels of alcohol, and low to substantial oak.
Grenache Rosé (Australia)
Grenache Rosé (France)
Grenache Rosé (USA)
Grignolino (Italy)
Other rosé blends (France, Portugal, Spain, USA)

WHITE WINES

Light-Bodied White Wines
Clean, refreshing wines with lower alcohol levels and little or no oak.
Albariño (Spain)
Arneis (Italy)
Chenin Blanc (France)
Chenin Blanc (South Africa)
Muscadet (France)
Pinot Blanc (France)
Pinot Blanc (Italy)
Pinot Grigio (Italy)
Pinot Grigio (USA)
Riesling (Austria)
Riesling (Germany)
Riesling (USA)
Sauvignon Blanc (France)
Sauvignon Blanc (New Zealand)
Sauvignon Blanc (South Africa)
Sauvignon Blanc (South America)
Sauvignon Blanc (USA)
Tocai (Italy)
Trebbiano (Italy)

Off-Dry White Wines
Light, refreshing wines with low alcohol and oak and a hint of sweetness.
Chenin Blanc (South Africa)
Chenin Blanc (USA)
Gewürztraminer (Austria)
Gewürztraminer (USA)
Muscat (Italy)
Riesling (Austria)
Riesling (Germany)
Riesling (USA)

Medium-Bodied White Wines
Fairly rich wines with moderate levels of alcohol and no, light, or moderate levels of oak.
Albariño (Spain)
Alvarinho (Portugal)
Chardonnay (France)
Chardonnay (Italy)
Chardonnay (South America)
Chardonnay (Spain)
Chardonnay (USA)
Chenin Blanc (France)
Frascati (Italy)
Gavi (Italy)
Orvieto (Italy)
Pinot Gris (France)
Pinot Gris (USA)
Riesling (Australia)
Sauvignon Blanc (France)
Sauvignon Blanc (New Zealand)
Sauvignon Blanc (USA)
Sémillon (Australia)
Sémillon (USA)
Vernaccia (Italy)

Full-Bodied White Wines
Rich wines with moderate to high levels of alcohol and light to heavy levels of oak.
Chardonnay (Australia)
Chardonnay (France)
Chardonnay (USA)
Sauvignon Blanc (New Zealand)
Sauvignon Blanc (USA)
Sémillon (Australia)
Sémillon (USA)

Big, Bold White Wines
Rich, robust white wines high in alcohol with possible use of oak.
Chardonnay (Australia)
Chardonnay (France)
Chardonnay (USA)
Greco (Italy)
Marsanne/blends (France)
Marsanne/blends (USA)
Pinot Gris (France)
Pinot Gris (USA)
Sémillon/blends (Australia)
Sémillon/blends (USA)
Viognier (France)
Viognier (USA)

RED WINES

Light-Bodied Red Wines

Simple, dry, fruity wines.

Barbera (Italy)
Cabernet/blends (Australia)
Cabernet/blends (France)
Cabernet/blends (Italy)
Cabernet/blends (South America)
Cabernet/blends (USA)
Carignan/blends (France)
Corvina (Italy)
Dolcetto (Italy)
Gamay (France)
Gamay Beaujolais (USA)
Merlot (France)
Merlot (Italy)
Merlot (South America)
Merlot (USA)
Napa Gamay (USA)
Pinot Noir (France)
Pinot Noir (USA)
Sangiovese/blends (Italy)
Sangiovese/blends (USA)

Medium-Bodied Red Wines

Reasonably rich, dry wines.

Barbera (Italy)
Cabernet/blends (Australia)
Cabernet/blends (France)
Cabernet/blends (Italy)
Cabernet/blends (South America)
Cabernet/blends (USA)
Carignan/blends (France)
Carignan/blends (Spain)
Carignan/blends (USA)
Corvina (Italy)
Dolcetto (Italy)
Gamay (France)
Gamay Beaujolais (USA)

Grenache/blends (France)
Grenache/blends (USA)
Merlot (France)
Merlot (Italy)
Merlot (South America)
Merlot (USA)
Nebbiolo (Italy)
Pinot Noir (France)
Pinot Noir (USA)
Sangiovese/blends (Italy)
Sangiovese/blends (USA)
Syrah/blends (Australia)
Syrah/blends (France)
Syrah/blends (USA)
Tempranillo (Spain)
Zinfandel (USA)

Full-Bodied Red Wines

Very rich, dry wines with significant use of oak.

Cabernet/blends (Australia)
Cabernet/blends (France)
Cabernet/blends (USA)
Carignan (North Africa)
Carignan/blends (France)
Mourvèdre (France)
Mourvèdre (USA)
Nebbiolo (Italy)
Petite Syrah (USA)
Pinotage (South Africa)
Rhône/blends (France)
Sangiovese/blends (Italy)
Syrah/blends (Australia)
Syrah/blends (France)
Syrah/blends (USA)
Tannat (France)
Tempranillo (Spain)
Zinfandel (USA)

DESSERT WINES

Sweet wines with varying levels of alcohol and oak.

Banyuls (France)

Champagne, extra-dry and demi-sec (France)

Chenin Blanc, late-harvest or botrytis (France)

Chenin Blanc, late-harvest or botrytis (USA)

Madeira, sweet styles (Spain)

Muscat, dessert style or sparkling (Italy)

Muscat, late-harvest or fortified (Australia)

Muscat, late-harvest or fortified (France)

Muscat, late-harvest or fortified (North Africa)

Muscat, late-harvest or fortified (USA)

Port (Australia)

Port (Great Britain)

Port (Portugal)

Port (USA)

Riesling, late-harvest or botrytis (France)

Riesling, late-harvest or botrytis (Germany)

Riesling, late-harvest or botrytis (USA)

Sémillon/blends, late-harvest or botrytis (France)

Sémillon/blends, late-harvest or botrytis (USA)

Sherry, sweet styles (Spain)

Sparkling wines, extra-dry and demi-sec (USA)

Tokay (Hungary)

Vin Santo (Italy)

Serving Wine

A terra-cotta wine bucket (above) has just the right insulation to keep a bottle of chilled white wine at its ideal serving temperature throughout a meal. To quickly chill a bottle of white wine that is at room temperature, place it in a nonporous container filled with equal amounts of ice cubes and water for 20–25 minutes.

Serving Temperatures

As a general rule, sparkling, white, rosé, and sweet dessert wines should be served at cooler temperatures than red wines. This holds true for two reasons: wines served cooler are regarded as more refreshing (although if they are served too cold, they lose their balance and complexity), and, on a more technical level, cold temperatures increase the harshness present in wines high in tannins—that is, heavy red wines. Some light red wines that are low in tannins, however, can be lovely when slightly chilled.

Use the following chart as a guide, serving wines at higher or lower temperatures in the given ranges according to your personal preference.

SPARKLING WINES: 40°–47°F (5°–8°C)

DRY WHITE WINES, ROSÉS: 44°–54°F (7°–12°C)

FULL WHITE WINES, LIGHT RED WINES: 50°–55°F (10°–13°C)

MEDIUM TO FULL RED WINES: 55°–65°F (13°–18°C)

DESSERT WINES: 41°–47°F (5°–8°C)

FORTIFIED DESSERT WINES: 55°–65°F (13°–18°C)

Choosing Glassware

While a number of different classic wineglass shapes (below) are available, they share a handful of basic attributes. To show off the wine's color and clarity to best advantage, they should be made of clear, unadorned glass. The bowls should be large enough to

Red Bordeaux   Red Burgundy   All-purpose Red   All-purpose Tasting

hold 3–4 fluid ounces (90–125 ml) of wine, while still leaving a generous empty space at the top in which the wine's bouquet can develop. Generally speaking, the rim of the glass should be slightly narrower than the bowl at its widest point, to help contain the bouquet. Glassware stems should be long enough to hold comfortably. This keeps fingers clear of the bowls so that they don't warm the wine or smudge the glass.

Saving Leftover Wine

The flavors of a leftover wine gradually change and dissipate upon contact with oxygen. You can, however, preserve the quality of the wine by using small canisters of inert gases (available in most wineshops) that can be sprayed into opened bottles to force out the air before they are recorked. You can also buy vacuum wine savers that include special reusable rubber stoppers through which the air is sucked out by a hand-operated pump.

To keep the bubbles in Champagne and other sparkling wines, buy a clamp-type stopper specifically designed to seal such bottles securely. Store any leftover still or sparkling wine in the refrigerator, and enjoy it within a few days of opening.

STORING WINE

While ideal cellar temperatures range from 55° to 57°F (13°–14°C), wines will be fine if stored at temperatures as high as 68°F (20°C). The important thing is to keep the bottles undisturbed and to avoid exposing them to extreme temperature fluctuations. Consider storing wine in the bottom of a closet or pantry, well away from heat sources and light.

To prevent corks from drying out and allowing air to enter, place the bottles on their sides. A wide variety of stackable storage racks such as the one shown below, are available in wineshops and kitchen-supply stores. They help make the storage of wine orderly and accessible.

All-purpose White   Sparkling Wine

Planning Menus

Designing a meal around a special bottle of wine can be enormously rewarding, because an appropriately chosen recipe or two often reveals something wonderful about the wine that you may not notice otherwise. Another way to approach your meal planning is to group recipes according to what is in season, a desired level of formality, or a favorite ethnic cuisine, all of which are illustrated in the menus presented here. For these meals, open some of the wines suggested for the selected recipes and experiment with the ideas discussed in their introductory notes. Give your guests as many glasses as there are wines and encourage them to discover their favorite food-and-wine combinations.

Autumn Feast

Fried Oysters with Classic
Tartar Sauce
PAGE 20

Hearty Beef Stew
PAGE 93

Caramelized Walnut Tart
PAGE 96

Italian Supper

Minestrone
PAGE 36

Sautéed Veal with
Prosciutto and Sage
PAGE 74

Almond Biscotti

Weekend Grill

Grilled Peppery Rib-Eye Steak
with Roquefort Butter
PAGE 90

Mixed Grilled Vegetables

Berry Crisp
PAGE 100

From the Sea

Tuna Tartare
PAGE 26

Seafood Curry with Coconut,
Citrus, and Cucumber
PAGE 51

Fresh Fruit

Family and Friends

Chicken with Ratatouille
PAGE 29

Tossed Green Salad

Warm Gingerbread
PAGE 107

Spring Celebration

Asparagus and Garlic
Omelet
PAGE 33

Roast Chicken with Rosemary,
Garlic, and Lemon
PAGE 48

Strawberries and Cream

Casual French

Onion and Olive Tart
PAGE 19

Coq au Vin
PAGE 85

Coffee Pôts de Crème
PAGE 103

Festive Entertaining

Deviled Crab Cakes
with Aioli
PAGE 25

Cornish Hens with
Grapes and Sage
PAGE 72

Chocolate Decadence Cake
PAGE 95

Exotic Flavors

Sautéed Scallops with Orange,
Fennel, and Ginger
PAGE 63

Indian Chicken Curry with
Coconut and Spiced Onions
PAGE 64

Sliced Mangoes

Dinner with Style

Corn Cakes with Smoked
Salmon and Crème Fraîche
PAGE 22

Lamb Chops with
Moroccan Spices
PAGE 71

Peach or Nectarine Gratin
PAGE 99

Onion and Olive Tart

PREP TIME: 50 MINUTES, PLUS 1 HOUR FOR CHILLING PASTRY

COOKING TIME: 1 HOUR

INGREDIENTS

FOR THE PASTRY

1½ cups (7½ oz/235 g) all-purpose (plain) flour

pinch of salt

½ cup (4 oz/125 g) chilled unsalted butter, cut into slivers

3–4 tablespoons ice water

FOR THE TAPENADE

½ cup (2½ oz/75 g) pitted Niçoise or Kalamata olives

1 tablespoon capers, rinsed

2 teaspoons chopped anchovy fillet

1 teaspoon minced garlic

1 teaspoon grated lemon zest

½ teaspoon ground pepper

2–3 tablespoons fruity olive oil

FOR THE FILLING

3 tablespoons unsalted butter

1 tablespoon olive oil

3 large yellow onions, cut into slices ¼ inch (6 mm) thick

2 tablespoons all-purpose (plain) flour

salt and ground pepper to taste

2 teaspoons chopped fresh thyme

1 cup (8 fl oz/250 ml) heavy (double) cream

2 eggs

½ cup (2 oz/60 g) shredded Gruyère or Emmentaler cheese

This luscious tart is a wine challenge. It requires enough acidity from the wine to balance the body and saltiness of the dish, yet not too much or its subtle richness is lost. Bubbly wines are ideal.

DEPENDABLE: PROSECCO FROM NORTHERN ITALY
DARING: SYRAH BLEND

SERVES 8

❋ To make the pastry, in a food processor, combine the flour and salt and pulse to combine. Add the butter and process until the mixture resembles cornmeal. Add 3 tablespoons ice water and process until the dough just holds together, adding the remaining 1 tablespoon if the mixture is too dry. Gather into a ball, place in plastic wrap, and refrigerate for at least 1 hour or for up to 3 days.

❋ To make the tapenade, in a food processor, combine the olives, capers, anchovy, garlic, lemon zest, pepper, and 2 tablespoons olive oil. Pulse to form a coarse purée, adding more oil if needed for spreadability.

❋ To make the filling, in a large sauté pan over medium heat, melt the butter with the oil. Add the onions and sauté, stirring occasionally, until very soft, about 20 minutes. Sprinkle with the flour, salt, and pepper and continue to cook, stirring, for 2 minutes. Add the thyme, stir briefly, and then let cool for 10 minutes. Meanwhile, in a small bowl, whisk together the cream and eggs. Season with salt and pepper.

❋ Preheat an oven to 425°F (220°C). On a lightly floured work surface, roll out the pastry into an 11-inch (28-cm) round. Carefully transfer to a 9-inch (23-cm) tart pan with a removable bottom. Trim the pastry even with the pan rim. Line the pastry shell with aluminum foil and fill with pie weights. Bake until slightly set, 10–15 minutes. Remove from the oven and remove the weights and foil. Let cool for 10 minutes. Reduce the oven temperature to 350°F (180°C).

❋ Spread the tapenade in the pastry shell. Top with the onions. Slowly pour in the cream mixture and sprinkle with the cheese. Bake until the custard is set, about 25 minutes. Let cool on a rack for about 10 minutes, then remove the pan sides and carefully slide the tart onto a serving plate. Serve warm.

NUTRITIONAL ANALYSIS PER SERVING: Calories 527 (Kilojoules 2,213); Protein 10 g; Carbohydrates 34 g; Total Fat 40 g; Saturated Fat 20 g; Cholesterol 145 mg; Sodium 274 mg; Dietary Fiber 3 g

Fried Oysters with Classic Tartar Sauce

PREP TIME: 25 MINUTES

COOKING TIME: 15 MINUTES

INGREDIENTS

FOR THE TARTAR SAUCE

¾ cup (6 fl oz/180 ml) mayonnaise

3 tablespoons finely minced white onion

2 tablespoons minced fresh chives

2 tablespoons chopped fresh flat-leaf (Italian) parsley

2 tablespoons minced cornichons, plus brine from jar, if needed

1 tablespoon coarsely chopped rinsed capers

1 tablespoon Creole or Dijon mustard

1 tablespoon lemon juice

salt and ground pepper to taste

24 oysters in the shell

peanut or vegetable oil for deep-frying

3 eggs

3 tablespoons heavy (double) cream or milk

1 cup (5 oz/155 g) all-purpose (plain) flour, or as needed

salt and ground pepper to taste

1 cup (4 oz/125 g) fine cracker crumbs, or as needed

COOKING TIP: This dish is at its best when you shuck the oysters just before cooking to keep them moist.

The toasty crunch, the rich fried surface, and the sprinkle of salt on these delectable oysters make a bubbly wine sparkle even more. You don't need a complex and expensive bottle here—simply dry and tart enough to counter the deep-fried flavor of the shellfish and the creaminess of the sauce.

DEPENDABLE: CAVA (DRY SPARKLING WINE FROM SPAIN)
DARING: FULL-BODIED, OAK-AGED CALIFORNIAN CHARDONNAY

SERVES 4

❀ To make the tartar sauce, in a bowl, combine the mayonnaise, white onion, chives, parsley, cornichons, capers, mustard, and lemon juice. Season with salt and pepper. Taste and adjust with liquid from the cornichons if more tartness is desired. Cover and refrigerate until needed.

❀ Grip each oyster, flat side up, with a folded kitchen towel. To one side of the hinge, push in the tip of an oyster knife and pry upward to open the shell. Run the knife blade all around the oyster to cut the muscle that holds the shell halves together. Discard the top shell. Run the knife underneath the oyster to cut its flesh free from the bottom shell, then discard the bottom shell.

❀ Line a baking sheet with parchment (baking) or waxed paper. Pour oil into a heavy sauté pan or cast-iron frying pan to a depth of 2 inches (5 cm) and heat to 375°F (190°C) on a deep-frying thermometer, or until the surface of the oil ripples.

❀ Meanwhile, in a small bowl, whisk together the eggs and cream or milk. Spread the flour on a plate and season lightly with salt and pepper. Spread the cracker crumbs on another plate. Dip each oyster in the flour, coating evenly, then in the egg mixture, and finally in the cracker crumbs. Set aside on the lined baking sheet until all are ready to fry.

❀ Slip the oysters into the hot oil, a few at a time, and fry until golden, 1–2 minutes. Using a slotted spoon or wire skimmer, transfer to paper towels to drain briefly. Sprinkle with salt.

❀ Arrange the oysters on a warmed platter or individual plates and serve immediately with the tartar sauce.

NUTRITIONAL ANALYSIS PER SERVING: Calories 801 (Kilojoules 3,364); Protein 18 g; Carbohydrates 54 g; Total Fat 57 g; Saturated Fat 17 g; Cholesterol 246 mg; Sodium 1,040 mg; Dietary Fiber 2 g

Corn Cakes with Smoked Salmon and Crème Fraîche

PREP TIME: 30 MINUTES

COOKING TIME: 15 MINUTES

INGREDIENTS

1¾ cups (10½ oz/330 g) white or yellow corn kernels (from about 2 ears)

⅓ cup (2 oz/60 g) fine yellow cornmeal

⅓ cup (2 oz/60 g) unbleached all-purpose (plain) flour

½ cup (4 fl oz/125 ml) milk

¼ cup (2 oz/60 g) unsalted butter, melted and cooled

2 eggs

½ teaspoon salt

¼ teaspoon ground pepper

¼ cup (2 fl oz/60 ml) melted clarified unsalted butter or peanut oil, or as needed

16 small slices smoked salmon

1 cup (8 fl oz/250 ml) crème fraîche

¼ cup (⅓ oz/10 g) snipped fresh chives

The crisp acidity of many dry sparkling wines is a refreshing counterpoint to the saltiness of smoked salmon. It also cuts through the richness that comes from frying these corn cakes and then serving them with crème fraîche. The accent of the corn adds an implied toastiness, which is a hallmark of many French Champagnes.

DEPENDABLE: NONVINTAGE FRENCH CHAMPAGNE
DARING: OFF-DRY RIESLING FROM GERMANY OR THE UNITED STATES

SERVES 4

❋ Place the corn kernels in a food processor. Using on-off pulses, pulse only until a coarse purée forms. Do not overprocess. Transfer to a bowl and whisk in the cornmeal and flour until smoothly incorporated.

❋ In another bowl, whisk together the milk, melted butter, and eggs until blended. Add to the corn mixture and stir to combine. Stir in the ½ teaspoon salt and ¼ teaspoon pepper. (The batter may be prepared up to a few hours before cooking, covered, and refrigerated.)

❋ Place a large nonstick or well-seasoned sauté pan or griddle over medium-high heat. When hot, brush with the clarified butter or peanut oil. Using about 2 tablespoons batter for each cake, ladle the batter onto the hot surface and spread to form cakes about 3 inches (7.5 cm) in diameter. The batter should sizzle when it hits the pan. Cook until golden on the first side, about 3 minutes. Then turn and cook on the second side until golden and the center is set, about 2 minutes longer. Transfer to a plate and keep warm until all the cakes are cooked.

❋ To serve, place 2 corn cakes on each warmed individual plate. Top each corn cake with 2 slices of smoked salmon, a generous drizzle of crème fraîche, and a sprinkling of chives. Serve immediately.

NUTRITIONAL ANALYSIS PER SERVING: Calories 759 (Kilojoules 3,188); Protein 27 g; Carbohydrates 40 g; Total Fat 55 g; Saturated Fat 32 g; Cholesterol 244 mg; Sodium 2,091 mg; Dietary Fiber 4 g

Deviled Crab Cakes with Aioli

PREP TIME: 30 MINUTES

COOKING TIME: 15 MINUTES,
   PLUS 15 MINUTES FOR
   COOLING ONIONS

INGREDIENTS

FOR THE AIOLI

2 teaspoons finely minced garlic

coarse salt to taste

I cup (8 fl oz/250 ml) mayonnaise

3 tablespoons lemon juice

I red bell pepper (capsicum), roasted,
   peeled, seeded, and puréed
   (optional)

FOR THE CRAB CAKES

2 tablespoons unsalted butter

I yellow onion, finely minced

2 celery stalks, chopped

2 teaspoons dry mustard

¼–½ teaspoon cayenne pepper

I lb (500 g) lump crabmeat, picked
   over for shell fragments

¼ cup (2 fl oz/60 ml) mayonnaise

I egg, lightly beaten

6 tablespoons (¾ oz/20 g) fresh
   bread crumbs

3 tablespoons chopped fresh flat-leaf
   (Italian) parsley

I teaspoon grated lemon zest

salt and ground black pepper to taste

I cup (4 oz/125 g) fine dried bread
   crumbs

2–4 tablespoons olive oil

While most crab cakes pair beautifully with light- or medium-bodied white wines, as soon as you introduce the element of cayenne pepper, you are looking at an ideal match for a sparkling wine. The effervescence takes the edge off the spiciness, and the textural contrast of fizz against the cakes' crispy crust is sublime. Also, the underlying tartness of the wine heightens the crab's natural sweetness.

DEPENDABLE: CALIFORNIAN BRUT SPARKLING WINE
DARING: GAMAY FROM FRANCE

SERVES 4

❀ To make the aioli, in a mortar, combine the garlic and coarse salt and grind together with a pestle to form a fine purée. Spoon the mayonnaise into a bowl and mix in the garlic purée and lemon juice. For red pepper aioli, fold in the roasted red pepper. Mix well, cover, and refrigerate until serving.

❀ To make the crab cakes, in a medium sauté pan over medium heat, melt the butter. Add the onion and celery and sauté until softened, about 5 minutes. Add the mustard and cayenne, stir well, and cook, stirring occasionally, about 2 minutes longer to blend in the spices. Transfer to a bowl and let cool to room temperature or refrigerate.

❀ When cool, stir in the crabmeat, mayonnaise, egg, fresh bread crumbs, parsley, and lemon zest. Season with salt and pepper.

❀ Spread the dried bread crumbs on a plate. Line a baking sheet with parchment (baking) or waxed paper. Divide the crab mixture into 4 or 8 equal portions, and shape each portion into a cake about ¾ inch (2 cm) thick. As each cake is formed, dip it in the bread crumbs, turning to coat completely, and then place it on the prepared baking sheet.

❀ In a large frying pan over medium-high heat, add enough olive oil to film the bottom lightly. When hot, add the crab cakes, a few at a time, and fry, turning once, until golden brown, 3–4 minutes on each side.

❀ Transfer to warmed individual plates and spoon a generous dollop of aioli on each plate or arrange on a platter. Serve immediately.

NUTRITIONAL ANALYSIS PER SERVING: Calories 929 (Kilojoules 3,902); Protein 31 g; Carbohydrates 33 g; Total Fat 76 g; Saturated Fat 14 g; Cholesterol 223 mg; Sodium 1,018 mg; Dietary Fiber 3 g

Tuna Tartare

PREP TIME: 20 MINUTES

INGREDIENTS

1 lb (500 g) sashimi-quality tuna fillet, preferably bigeye or yellowfin, cut into ¼-inch (6-mm) dice

¼ cup (1½ oz/45 g) finely minced red (Spanish) onion

1½ tablespoons minced green or red jalapeño chile, seeded if desired

2 tablespoons finely minced green (spring) onion, including tender green tops

2 teaspoons grated lemon zest

¼ cup (2 fl oz/60 ml) olive oil

3 tablespoons Asian sesame oil

kosher or sea salt and coarsely ground pepper to taste

1 lemon, quartered

Here is a beautiful scenario for color coding: rosé sparkling wine against the rich red tones of tuna tartare. The oily flesh of the tuna needs just a bit of balancing, which the wine's acidity provides, as it subtly enhances the lemon. To echo the toastiness of the wine, serve this spicy dish with toasted French bread or with quickly fried pappadams from India.

DEPENDABLE: DRY ROSÉ CHAMPAGNE OR SPARKLING WINE
DARING: OFF-DRY WHITE WINE SUCH AS CHENIN BLANC

SERVES 4

✤ In a bowl, carefully and gently combine the tuna, red onion, chile, green onion, lemon zest, olive oil, and sesame oil. Season generously with salt and pepper.

✤ Mound the tuna mixture on individual plates and serve immediately with lemon wedges.

NUTRITIONAL ANALYSIS PER SERVING: Calories 345 (Kilojoules 1,450); Protein 27 g; Carbohydrates 5 g; Total Fat 25 g; Saturated Fat 4 g; Cholesterol 51 mg; Sodium 45 mg; Dietary Fiber 0 g

Chicken with Ratatouille

PREP TIME: 45 MINUTES,
PLUS 30 MINUTES FOR
DRAINING EGGPLANT

COOKING TIME: 1 HOUR

INGREDIENTS

1 lb (500 g) Asian (slender) eggplants (aubergines), unpeeled, cut
into slices 1 inch (2.5 cm) thick,
or 1 globe eggplant (aubergine),
about 1 lb (500 g), peeled and cut
into 1-inch (2.5-cm) cubes

salt

1 chicken, about 4 lb (2 kg), cut into
small serving pieces

ground pepper to taste

6 tablespoons (3 fl oz/90 ml) olive oil,
or as needed

2 yellow or red (Spanish) onions,
sliced or coarsely chopped

2 green or red bell peppers (cap-
sicums), seeded and cut into
long, narrow strips or 1-inch
(2.5-cm) squares

1½ lb (750 g) tomatoes, peeled,
seeded, and chopped

4 small zucchini (courgettes), about
1 lb (500 g), cut into ½-inch
(12-mm) chunks

1 bay leaf

2 tablespoons chopped fresh thyme,
marjoram, or basil, plus extra for
garnish (optional)

3 cloves garlic, minced

½ cup (4 fl oz/125 ml) dry white wine

The mixture of robust vegetables in ratatouille cries out for both the spiciness of a red wine and the refreshment of a white wine, so try a rosé. Look for a wine as tart as the tomatoes and as complex as the unctuous mixture of onions, garlic, eggplant, peppers, and zucchini. A Grenache rosé adds a pleasant peppery characteristic to the combination. Serve the chicken with rice or mashed potatoes.

DEPENDABLE: GRENACHE ROSÉ FROM FRANCE OR AUSTRALIA
DARING: LIGHT-BODIED MERLOT FROM WASHINGTON, ITALY, OR CHILE

SERVES 4

❂ Sprinkle the eggplant slices or cubes with salt and place in a colander. Let stand for about 30 minutes to drain off the bitter juices. Rinse and pat dry with paper towels. Set aside.

❂ Rinse the chicken pieces and pat dry with paper towels. Sprinkle with salt and pepper.

❂ In a large, heavy sauté pan over high heat, warm 3 tablespoons of the olive oil. Add the chicken pieces and turn to brown on all sides, about 10 minutes. Using tongs or a slotted spoon, transfer the chicken pieces to a plate. Reduce the heat to medium.

❂ To the oil remaining in the pan, add the onions and sauté, stirring occasionally, until softened and translucent, about 8 minutes. Add 3 more tablespoons of the olive oil to the pan, then add the eggplant and cook, turning as needed, until lightly browned, 8–10 minutes. Add the bell peppers and cook, stirring often, until softened, about 5 minutes longer. Add the tomatoes, zucchini, bay leaf, 2 tablespoons chopped herbs, garlic, and wine, and simmer until well blended, about 5 minutes.

❂ Return the chicken pieces to the pan, tossing and stirring to mix with the vegetables. Cover, reduce the heat to low, and simmer gently until the chicken is tender, 20–25 minutes.

❂ Season with salt and pepper and transfer to a warmed serving dish. Sprinkle with additional chopped herbs, if you like, and serve at once.

NUTRITIONAL ANALYSIS PER SERVING: Calories 940 (Kilojoules 3,950); Protein 62 g; Carbohydrates 22 g; Total Fat 68 g; Saturated Fat 16 g; Cholesterol 232 mg; Sodium 239 mg; Dietary Fiber 5 g

Paella

PREP TIME: 1 HOUR, PLUS
  OVERNIGHT FOR MARINAT-
  ING CHICKEN

COOKING TIME: 50 MINUTES

INGREDIENTS

4 each small chicken thighs and
  breast halves

1½ tablespoons finely minced garlic

1½ tablespoons dried oregano

2 teaspoons coarsely ground pepper

1 teaspoon salt

3 tablespoons red wine vinegar

5 tablespoons (2½ fl oz/75 ml) extra-
  virgin olive oil

½ teaspoon saffron threads

¼ cup (2 fl oz/60 ml) dry white wine

6 oz (185 g) chorizo sausages

6 tablespoons (3 fl oz/90 ml) olive oil

2 yellow onions, chopped

2–3 cups (12–18 oz/375–560 g)
  peeled, seeded, and diced tomatoes (fresh or canned)

1 tablespoon minced garlic

1½ cups (10½ oz/330 g) short-grain
  white rice

4 cups (32 fl oz/1 l) chicken broth,
  or as needed

16 shrimp (prawns), peeled and
  deveined

1 cup (5 oz/155 g) shelled English
  peas, blanched in boiling water for
  1 minute and drained

24 clams or mussels, well scrubbed
  and mussels debearded

Light- to medium-bodied spicy reds, such as a Spanish Rioja, are traditional with this dish, but a rosé can be equally stellar. One based on aromatic, spicy grapes like Tempranillo is best.

DEPENDABLE: SPANISH ROSÉ BASED ON TEMPRANILLO
DARING: BOLD CHARDONNAY FROM SPAIN OR PORTUGAL

SERVES 4

❁ Rinse the chicken pieces and pat dry. In a small bowl, stir together the garlic, oregano, pepper, and salt. Stir in the vinegar to form a paste. Stir in the extra-virgin olive oil. Rub the paste on the chicken and place in a nonaluminum container. Cover and refrigerate overnight.

❁ Crumble the saffron into a small saucepan, add the wine, and bring to a simmer. Remove from the heat and let steep for 10 minutes. In a frying pan over medium-high heat, sauté the sausages until golden brown, about 5 minutes. Cut into 1-inch (2.5-cm) chunks and set aside.

❁ In a large frying pan over high heat, warm 3–4 tablespoons (1½–2 fl oz/ 45–60 ml) of the olive oil. Add the marinated chicken pieces and brown on all sides, about 10 minutes. Using tongs, transfer to a plate. Wipe out the pan. Add the remaining 2–3 tablespoons oil and place over medium heat. Add the onions and sauté until soft, about 10 minutes. Add the tomatoes and garlic and cook, stirring occasionally, until blended, about 5 minutes. Add the rice and stir until opaque, about 3 minutes. Raise the heat to high, add 4 cups (32 fl oz/1 l) broth, or as needed to cover well, and the saffron and wine. Bring to a boil, reduce the heat to low, and simmer, uncovered, until the rice is half cooked, about 10 minutes. Return the chicken to the pan and cook until most of the liquid has been absorbed and the chicken is cooked through, about 10 minutes longer. Stir in the shrimp, sausages, and peas during the final 5–8 minutes of cooking; the shrimp will be pink when ready.

❁ Meanwhile, in a wide saucepan, pour water to a depth of 1 inch (2.5 cm). Add the clams or mussels, discarding any that do not close to the touch, cover, and place over medium-high heat. Steam, shaking the pan occasionally, until the shellfish open, 3–5 minutes. Discard any that fail to open. Stir the clams or mussels and their pan juices into the paella. Let stand for 10 minutes before serving.

NUTRITIONAL ANALYSIS PER SERVING: Calories 1,354 (Kilojoules 5,687); Protein 78 g; Carbohydrates 85 g; Total Fat 77 g; Saturated Fat 19 g; Cholesterol 264 mg; Sodium 2,444 mg; Dietary Fiber 5 g

Asparagus and Garlic Omelet

PREP TIME: 15 MINUTES

COOKING TIME: 30 MINUTES

INGREDIENTS

½ lb (250 g) pencil-thin asparagus
spears

4 tablespoons (2 fl oz/60 ml) olive oil

2 shallots, finely chopped, or 6 green
(spring) onions, including tender
green tops, finely chopped

8 fresh garlic chives, snipped

2 cloves garlic, finely minced

4 extra-large eggs or 5 large eggs

salt and ground pepper to taste

PREP TIP: While you can season the
omelet with a combination of garlic
chives and fresh garlic, if you are
able to find green garlic at the start
of spring, you will have an even
more fragrant dish.

Eggs and asparagus are challenging foods to pair with wine. Eggs coat the mouth and allow very little wine flavor to show. Asparagus has a strong grassy, vegetal taste, which dominates most wines. But there are wines capable of standing up to both eggs and asparagus, namely Muscadets. The omelet is a perfect first course or part of a tapa assortment; or, served in a larger portion, a delightful lunch or light supper. For a more substantial dish, sauté ¼ pound (125 g) peeled and deveined shrimp (prawns) or picked over lump crabmeat with the asparagus.

DEPENDABLE: TART, YOUTHFUL MUSCADET
DARING: GRENACHE OR SYRAH BLEND SUCH AS CHÂTEAUNEUF-DU-PAPE

SERVES 4

❀ Trim off the tough ends from the asparagus and cut the spears into 1-inch (2.5-cm) lengths. Bring a saucepan three-fourths full of water to a boil, add the asparagus, and parboil for 3 minutes. Drain, rinse with cold water, drain again, and pat dry.

❀ In a medium sauté pan over low heat, warm 2 tablespoons of the olive oil. Add the shallots or green onions and sauté until softened, about 8 minutes. Add the chives, garlic, and asparagus and sauté, stirring, until the asparagus is tender, about 2 minutes. Remove from the heat.

❀ In a bowl, whisk the eggs until blended. Add the asparagus mixture and season with salt and pepper.

❀ In an 8-inch (20-cm) omelet or sauté pan over high heat, warm the remaining 2 tablespoons olive oil. When very hot, pour in the egg mixture and immediately reduce the heat to medium. Cook, running a spatula around the edges of the pan a few times, until the underside is golden, 8–10 minutes. Invert a flat plate on top of the pan and, holding the plate and pan together firmly, carefully invert them. Lift off the pan, slide the omelet back into it, browned side up, and return to medium heat. Cook on the second side just until pale gold, about 4 minutes longer. Do not overcook, as you don't want the omelet to dry out.

❀ Slide onto a serving plate, let cool a bit, and then cut into wedges.

NUTRITIONAL ANALYSIS PER SERVING: Calories 221 (Kilojoules 928); Protein 9 g; Carbohydrates 4 g; Total Fat 19 g; Saturated Fat 4 g; Cholesterol 245 mg; Sodium 74 mg; Dietary Fiber 1 g

Pasta with Green Beans, Potatoes, and Pesto

PREP TIME: 40 MINUTES

COOKING TIME: 40 MINUTES

INGREDIENTS

FOR THE PESTO

¼ cup (2 oz/60 g) pine nuts or walnuts

2 cups (3 oz/90 g) tightly packed fresh basil leaves

2 or 3 cloves garlic

¼ cup (1 oz/30 g) grated pecorino sardo or Parmesan cheese

½ cup (4 fl oz/125 ml) extra-virgin olive oil, or as needed

salt and ground pepper to taste

8 new potatoes, 9–10 oz (280–315 g) total weight

4 tablespoons (2 fl oz/60 ml) extra-virgin olive oil

salt and ground pepper to taste

½ lb (250 g) green beans, trimmed and cut into 1–1½-inch (2.5–4-cm) lengths

1 lb (500 g) fresh tagliarini or fettuccine

¼ cup (1 oz/30 g) grated pecorino sardo or Parmesan cheese

MAKE-AHEAD TIP: The pesto can be made up to 5 days in advance. Transfer to a container, pour a thin layer of olive oil on top to prevent discoloring, cover, and refrigerate. Bring to room temperature before using.

Pesto is perhaps the world's greatest food for showing off light, leafy white wines. While a Sauvignon Blanc will certainly enhance the pesto and the beans, any other lightly herbal white wine will also do the trick. The addition of potatoes and pasta adds richness, which must be "cut," so look for a wine with noticeable acidity.

DEPENDABLE: SAUVIGNON BLANC
DARING: DRY SPARKLING WINE SUCH AS A PROSECCO

SERVES 4

❀ To make the pesto, preheat an oven to 350°F (180°C). Spread the nuts on a baking sheet and toast until they take on color and are fragrant, 5–8 minutes. Let cool. Leave the oven set at 350°F (180°C). In a food processor, combine the nuts, basil, and garlic. Pulse until the basil is chopped. Add the cheese and pulse to combine. With the motor running, pour in the ½ cup (4 fl oz/125 ml) oil, a few drops at a time, until the mixture has the consistency of mayonnaise, adding more oil as needed. Season with salt and pepper; set aside.

❀ Rub the new potatoes with 2 tablespoons of the olive oil, then season with salt and pepper. Place in a baking dish and roast, shaking the dish from time to time, until tender when pierced, about 35 minutes.

❀ Meanwhile, bring a large pot three-fourths full of salted water to a boil. Add the beans and cook until tender, about 4 minutes. Scoop out with a skimmer, cool under running water, and drain.

❀ Remove the potatoes from the oven and cut into bite-sized pieces. In a large sauté pan over high heat, warm the remaining 2 tablespoons olive oil. Add the potatoes and sauté until golden, about 4 minutes. Add the beans and stir until heated through, about 1 minute. Keep warm.

❀ Meanwhile, return the large pot of water to a boil. Drop in the pasta, stir well, and cook until al dente (tender, but firm to the bite), about 2 minutes. Drain, reserving a few tablespoons of the cooking water. Transfer to a warmed serving bowl.

❀ Stir the pesto and the reserved water into the vegetables in the pan (off the heat). Add to the pasta and toss well. Pass the cheese at the table.

NUTRITIONAL ANALYSIS PER SERVING: Calories 894 (Kilojoules 3,755); Protein 24 g; Carbohydrates 82 g; Total Fat 56 g; Saturated Fat 10 g; Cholesterol 92 mg; Sodium 654 mg; Dietary Fiber 7 g

Minestrone

PREP TIME: 30 MINUTES, PLUS
1 HOUR FOR SOAKING
BEANS

COOKING TIME: 1¾ HOURS

INGREDIENTS

½ cup (3½ oz/105 g) dried small
white beans or 1 can (15 oz/470 g)
white beans

salt to taste

2 tablespoons olive oil

2 yellow onions, diced

½ cup (3 oz/90 g) diced pancetta

3 carrots, peeled, halved lengthwise
if large, and thinly sliced

2 celery stalks, diced

¾ lb (375 g) tomatoes, peeled,
seeded, and diced

5–6 cups (40–48 fl oz/1.25–1.5 l)
water or chicken broth, or as
needed

4 small new potatoes, unpeeled,
diced

2 zucchini (courgettes), halved
lengthwise and sliced

¼ lb (125 g) green beans, trimmed
and cut into 1-inch (2.5-cm) lengths

2 cups (4 oz/125 g) chopped Swiss
chard (optional)

¼ lb (125 g) macaroni or small shells

2 tablespoons extra-virgin olive oil

ground pepper to taste

¼ cup (2 oz/60 g) pesto (page 35)

¼ cup (1 oz/30 g) grated Parmesan
cheese

Soup and wine don't marry well when the combination is simply broth against liquid. When the soup has ample flavor and texture, as is the case here, however, the wine is a pleasant point of difference. The "green" flavors of the zucchini, green beans, chard, and pesto call for an assertive Sauvignon Blanc.

DEPENDABLE: SAUVIGNON BLANC FROM NEW ZEALAND OR CALIFORNIA
DARING: LIGHTLY HERBAL MERLOT

SERVES 4

❀ If using dried beans, pick over and discard any misshapen beans or stones. Rinse, drain, and place in a pot with water to cover by 2 inches (5 cm). Bring to a boil, boil for 2 minutes, then cover, remove from the heat, and let stand for 1 hour. Drain and return to the pot with fresh water to cover by 2 inches (5 cm). Bring to a boil, reduce the heat to low, cover, and simmer until tender, 45–60 minutes. Add salt during the last 10 minutes of cooking. If using canned beans, drain and rinse well.

❀ In a large soup pot over medium heat, warm the olive oil. Add the onions and cook, stirring, until softened and translucent, about 10 minutes. Add the pancetta and cook, stirring, until tender, about 5 minutes longer. Add the carrots and celery and cook, stirring, until beginning to soften, just a few minutes. Add the tomatoes and enough water or broth to cover amply. Bring to a boil, reduce the heat to low, cover, and simmer until the tomatoes break down, about 10 minutes.

❀ Meanwhile, if desired, place half of the white beans in a food processor or blender with a little of the cooking liquid or, if using canned beans, a little stock. Purée until smooth.

❀ Add the potatoes, zucchini, green beans, white beans (including puréed, if using), Swiss chard (if using), and pasta and simmer until the vegetables and pasta are cooked, about 15 minutes. Stir often to prevent sticking. Swirl in the 2 tablespoons extra-virgin olive oil. Season with salt and pepper.

❀ Remove from the heat and stir in the pesto. Ladle into warmed bowls and serve immediately. Pass the Parmesan at the table.

NUTRITIONAL ANALYSIS PER SERVING: Calories 643 (Kilojoules 2,700); Protein 22 g; Carbohydrates 71 g; Total Fat 33 g; Saturated Fat 7 g; Cholesterol 19 mg; Sodium 438 mg; Dietary Fiber 11 g

Risotto with Artichokes

PREP TIME: 30 MINUTES

COOKING TIME: 50 MINUTES

INGREDIENTS

juice of 1 lemon

4–6 large artichokes

¼ cup (2 fl oz/60 ml) olive oil

1 yellow onion, chopped

1 teaspoon minced garlic

pinch of dried oregano (optional)

1 cup (8 fl oz/250 ml) water, or as needed

4 cups (32 fl oz/1 l) vegetable or chicken broth

6 tablespoons (3 oz/90 g) unsalted butter

1½ cups (10½ oz/330 g) Arborio rice

½ cup (4 fl oz/125 ml) dry white wine

salt and ground pepper to taste

¼ cup (1 oz/30 g) grated Parmesan cheese, plus extra for passing (optional)

Artichokes have the reputation of being difficult to pair with wine. Sometimes they make red wines taste bitter and whites seem oddly sweet. There are, however, two ways to work with them: overpower them with a tannic, herbal red, or better yet, choose a crisp, very dry Sauvignon Blanc.

DEPENDABLE: GRASSY AND HERBAL SAUVIGNON BLANC
DARING: LEAFY CABERNET FRANC

SERVES 4

❁ Have ready a large bowl three-fourths full of water to which you have added the lemon juice. Working with 1 artichoke at a time, trim off the stem flush with the bottom. If the stem has any tenderness, peel it lightly and cut into slices ⅓ inch (9 mm) thick. Drop the slices into the lemon water. Snap off all the leaves from the artichoke until only the tender heart remains. Cut lengthwise into quarters. Cut away the prickly choke and drop the artichoke pieces into the lemon water.

❁ In a sauté pan over medium heat, warm the olive oil. Add the onion and sauté until softened and translucent, about 8 minutes. Drain the artichokes and add to the pan along with the garlic, oregano (if using), and enough water to just cover the artichokes. Simmer, uncovered, until tender, 8–10 minutes. Remove from the heat and set aside.

❁ Pour the broth into a saucepan and place over medium-high heat. Bring to a simmer and adjust the heat to maintain a very gentle simmer. In a wide sauté pan over medium heat, melt 2 tablespoons of the butter. Add the rice and stir until opaque, about 4 minutes. Add the white wine and stir until absorbed. Add a ladleful of the simmering broth and stir until the broth is absorbed. Reduce the heat to low and continue to add the broth, a ladleful at a time, stirring until absorbed before adding more. The rice is cooked when the rice grains are al dente (tender, but still firm to the bite) at the center and creamy on the outside, 20–25 minutes total. Stir in the artichoke mixture with the last addition of broth.

❁ When the rice is done, stir in the remaining 4 tablespoons (2 oz/60 g) butter, season with salt and pepper, and remove from the heat. Sprinkle with the ¼ cup (1 oz/30 g) cheese. Transfer to a warmed serving bowl and serve. Pass additional cheese at the table, if desired.

NUTRITIONAL ANALYSIS PER SERVING: Calories 699 (Kilojoules 2,936); Protein 15 g; Carbohydrates 83 g; Total Fat 35 g; Saturated Fat 14 g; Cholesterol 51 mg; Sodium 1,297 mg; Dietary Fiber 13 g

Roast Pork Loin with Tarragon, Mustard, and Cream

PREP TIME: 20 MINUTES

COOKING TIME: 1¼ HOURS

INGREDIENTS

1 bone-in pork loin, 3–4 lb (1.5–2 kg)

3 large cloves garlic, slivered

salt and ground pepper to taste

¼ cup (2 oz/60 g) unsalted butter

3 tablespoons minced shallot

½ cup (4 fl oz/125 ml) chicken broth

2–3 tablespoons strong Dijon mustard

1 cup (8 fl oz/250 ml) heavy (double) cream

2–3 tablespoons chopped fresh tarragon

Pork is inherently sweet, a characteristic intensified by roasting. Cream is faintly sweet also. An off-dry white wine is the ideal partner for this combination, particularly if the wine has a nice counterbalance of acidity, which matches the tartness of the mustard, and carries just a hint of herbal flavor to echo the tarragon. Accompany the pork loin with sautéed apples and fried or roasted potatoes.

DEPENDABLE: OFF-DRY AMERICAN RIESLING
DARING: MEDIUM-BODIED MERLOT

SERVES 4

❀ Preheat an oven to 400°F (200°C).

❀ With the tip of a sharp knife, cut ¾-inch (2-cm) slits all over the pork loin. Insert the garlic slivers into the slits. Sprinkle the meat with salt and pepper and place in a roasting pan.

❀ Roast until an instant-read thermometer inserted into the thickest part of the loin away from the bone registers 147°–150°F (64°–65°C) or the meat is pale pink when cut in the thickest portion, about 1 hour. Transfer to a cutting board and let rest while you make the sauce.

❀ In a sauté pan over low heat, melt the butter. Add the shallot and sauté slowly until soft, about 5 minutes. Add the chicken broth and let cook until almost totally evaporated, about 5 minutes. Whisk in 2 tablespoons of the mustard and the cream and simmer until the sauce is slightly thickened, about 5 minutes. Stir in 2 tablespoons of the tarragon and season with salt and pepper. Taste and adjust the seasonings with more mustard or tarragon. Remove from the heat and keep warm.

❀ Carve the pork into chops with the bone and arrange on a warmed platter or individual plates. Spoon the sauce over the slices and serve immediately.

NUTRITIONAL ANALYSIS PER SERVING: Calories 923 (Kilojoules 3,876); Protein 67 g; Carbohydrates 4 g; Total Fat 69 g; Saturated Fat 34 g; Cholesterol 308 mg; Sodium 502 mg; Dietary Fiber 0 g

Grilled Fish in a Spicy Citrus Marinade

PREP TIME: 25 MINUTES, PLUS
2 HOURS FOR MARINATING

COOKING TIME: 10 MINUTES,
PLUS PREPARING FIRE

INGREDIENTS

4 firm, mild white fish fillets such as
   grouper, sea bass, flounder, cod,
   or halibut, about 6 oz (185 g) each

sea salt or kosher salt to taste

1 small yellow onion, diced

1 walnut-sized piece fresh ginger,
   peeled and thinly sliced

1 small bunch fresh cilantro (fresh
   coriander), chopped

1 tablespoon chopped garlic

2 teaspoons minced jalapeño chile

2 teaspoons grated lime zest

1 teaspoon ground pepper

¼ cup (2 fl oz/60 ml) lime juice

¼ cup (2 fl oz/60 ml) olive oil

1 lime, quartered (optional)

The goal of the wine here is to mitigate the chiles while bringing out the zesty nature of the lime and the sharpness of the ginger. Off-dry whites, especially those low in alcohol, which has a tendency to make chiles burn even more, do the trick. These subtly sweet wines also balance well with caramelized, smoky flavors from the grill. A plate of simply sautéed greens or a dish of black or red beans and rice will round out the menu.

DEPENDABLE: OFF-DRY GERMAN RIESLING
DARING: LIGHTLY OAK-AGED PINOT NOIR

SERVES 4

❀ Place the fish fillets in a nonaluminum container and sprinkle lightly with salt. In a food processor, combine the onion, ginger, cilantro, garlic, chile, lime zest, pepper, lime juice, and olive oil. Using on-off pulses, pulse until a paste forms. Rub the paste evenly over both sides of each fish fillet. Cover and marinate in the refrigerator for at least 2 hours or for up to 4 hours.

❀ Prepare a fire in a charcoal grill or preheat a broiler (griller).

❀ Sprinkle the fish fillets with salt again. Place on the oiled grill rack or on an oiled rack on a broiler pan and slip under the broiler. Grill or broil, turning once, until opaque throughout when pierced with a knife, 3–4 minutes on each side.

❀ Transfer to warmed individual plates. Serve immediately, with lime wedges if desired.

NUTRITIONAL ANALYSIS PER SERVING: Calories 300 (Kilojoules 1,260); Protein 34 g; Carbohydrates 6 g; Total Fat 15 g; Saturated Fat 2 g; Cholesterol 63 mg; Sodium 97 mg; Dietary Fiber 1 g

Grilled Chicken in a North African Marinade

PREP TIME: 25 MINUTES,
PLUS OVERNIGHT FOR
MARINATING

COOKING TIME: 15 MINUTES,
PLUS PREPARING FIRE

INGREDIENTS

2 tablespoons aniseed

¼ cup (⅓ oz/10 g) chopped fresh cilantro (fresh coriander)

¼ cup (¾ oz/20 g) chopped green (spring) onion, including tender green tops

4 cloves garlic, chopped

2 teaspoons paprika

2 teaspoons ground coriander

1 teaspoon ground ginger

1 teaspoon ground cinnamon

½ teaspoon saffron threads, finely chopped

½ teaspoon cayenne pepper

¼ cup (2 fl oz/60 ml) lemon juice

2 tablespoons honey

½ cup (4 fl oz/125 ml) olive oil, or as needed

ground black pepper to taste

2 broiler chickens, each about 2½ lb (1.25 kg), split

salt to taste

The wine should subtly bring out the exotic character of the aromatics (anise, saffron, ginger, and cinnamon) in this spicy grilled chicken. A fruity Gewürztraminer with a kiss of sweetness will do just that. Serve with couscous, a lemon wedge, and assorted grilled vegetables.

DEPENDABLE: OFF-DRY GEWÜRZTRAMINER
DARING: SPICY, PEPPERY ZINFANDEL

SERVES 4

❀ In a small sauté pan over medium heat, toast the aniseed, shaking the pan often, until fragrant, 3–4 minutes. Remove from the heat, let cool slightly, and transfer to a mortar. Grind coarsely with a pestle and transfer to a food processor. Add the cilantro, green onion, garlic, paprika, coriander, ginger, cinnamon, saffron, and cayenne pepper. Using on-off pulses, pulse to combine. Add the lemon juice and honey and again pulse to combine. The mixture should be pasty. Transfer to a bowl and whisk in ½ cup (4 fl oz/125 ml) olive oil until well incorporated, adding more as needed to coat. Season with generous grindings of black pepper. The marinade should be good and spicy.

❀ Rinse the chickens and pat dry with paper towels. Place in a non-aluminum container and coat evenly with the marinade. Cover and refrigerate overnight.

❀ Prepare a fire in a charcoal grill or preheat a broiler (griller).

❀ Bring the chicken to room temperature. Sprinkle the chicken with salt and place, skin side up, on the oiled grill rack or skin side down on the oiled rack of a broiler pan. Grill or broil until well browned, about 6 minutes. Turn and continue to grill or broil until the skin is well browned and caramelized and the meat is cooked through, 5–6 minutes longer. The juices should run clear when a leg is pierced with a skewer.

❀ Transfer to a warmed platter or individual plates and serve immediately.

NUTRITIONAL ANALYSIS PER SERVING: Calories 747 (Kilojoules 3,137); Protein 69 g; Carbohydrates 7 g; Total Fat 48 g; Saturated Fat 11 g; Cholesterol 220 mg; Sodium 209 mg; Dietary Fiber 0 g

Fish with Olives, Pine Nuts, Basil, and Wine

PREP TIME: 10 MINUTES

COOKING TIME: 25 MINUTES

INGREDIENTS

¼ cup (1 oz/30 g) pine nuts

4 firm white fish fillets such as snapper, rock cod, flounder, sea bass, halibut, or swordfish, 6–7 oz (185–220 g) each

kosher salt and ground pepper to taste

4 tablespoons (2 fl oz/60 ml) extra-virgin olive oil

⅓ cup (3 fl oz/80 ml) dry white wine

1½ tablespoons finely minced garlic

5 tablespoons (⅓ oz/10 g) fresh basil leaves, shredded

½ cup (2½ oz/75 g) Mediterranean-style green and/or black olives, pitted if desired

The bright fruit and moderately rich texture of a French Chardonnay harmonize magnificently with this Mediterranean dish. Search for one with a pungency similar to that of the olives and enough assertiveness to balance with the basil. If artichokes are in season, 2 artichoke hearts, steamed, sliced, and sautéed in olive oil, can be added with the olives. The same wine can still be served.

DEPENDABLE: FRENCH CHARDONNAY
DARING: BRIGHT ITALIAN WHITE SUCH AS SOAVE

SERVES 4

✸ Preheat an oven to 350°F (180°C). Spread the nuts on a baking sheet and toast in the oven until they take on color and are fragrant, 5–8 minutes. Remove from the oven and set aside. Raise the oven temperature to 400°F (200°C).

✸ Sprinkle the fish fillets with salt and pepper. Place in a baking dish in which they fit in a single layer. In a small bowl, stir together 3 tablespoons of the olive oil and the wine. Pour over the fish fillets. Top with half of the garlic and half of the basil, and then distribute the olives around the fillets. Cover with aluminum foil.

✸ Bake until the fish is opaque throughout when pierced with a knife, 10–15 minutes. The timing will depend upon the thickness of the fillets. Using a slotted spatula, transfer the fillets to warmed individual plates.

✸ Pour the pan juices, olives, and reserved pine nuts into a small sauté pan over medium heat and swirl in the remaining 1 tablespoon olive oil and the remaining garlic and basil. When warm and fragrant, spoon over the fish. Serve immediately.

NUTRITIONAL ANALYSIS PER SERVING: Calories 420 (Kilojoules 1,760); Protein 40 g; Carbohydrates 4 g; Total Fat 26 g; Saturated Fat 4 g; Cholesterol 68 mg; Sodium 702 mg; Dietary Fiber 1 g

Roast Chicken with Rosemary, Garlic, and Lemon

PREP TIME: 20 MINUTES

COOKING TIME: 1¼ HOURS,
  PLUS 15 MINUTES FOR
  RESTING

INGREDIENTS

1 roasting chicken, preferably free
  range, 4–4½ lb (2–2.25 kg)

1 lemon, quartered

kosher salt and ground pepper to
  taste

8 cloves garlic, crushed

4 fresh rosemary sprigs

⅓ cup (3 fl oz/80 ml) extra-virgin
  olive oil

¼ cup (2 fl oz/60 ml) lemon juice

1 teaspoon coarsely ground pepper

½ teaspoon table salt

A soft-textured Sauvignon Blanc and several medium-bodied white wines are often better than light reds with roasted chicken because they more fully complement the sweetness that develops during the roasting. If the wine has a citrusy edge, it nicely accentuates the lemon and herb flavors in the chicken. Serve with mashed potatoes and glazed carrots.

DEPENDABLE: SAUVIGNON BLANC BLEND WITH SOME SÉMILLON
DARING: CITRUS-SCENTED PINOT NOIR FROM OREGON OR CALIFORNIA

SERVES 4

❀ Preheat an oven to 375°F (190°C).

❀ Rinse the chicken and pat dry with paper towels. Rub inside and out with the cut sides of the lemon quarters. Then rub with kosher salt and ground pepper. Place the lemon quarters, 4 of the garlic cloves, and 2 of the rosemary sprigs in the cavity of the chicken. Place, breast side up, on a lightly oiled rack in a roasting pan.

❀ Chop the remaining garlic coarsely. Remove the needles from the remaining rosemary sprigs and chop coarsely.

❀ In a small saucepan over medium heat, combine the chopped garlic and rosemary, the olive oil, lemon juice, coarsely ground pepper, and table salt. Bring to a simmer and simmer until aromatic, about 3 minutes. Remove from the heat.

❀ Roast the chicken, basting with the olive oil mixture every 15 minutes, until an instant-read thermometer inserted into the thickest part of the thigh away from the bone registers 180°F (82°C) or the juices run clear when the thigh joint is pierced, about 1¼ hours.

❀ Transfer the chicken to a cutting board and cover loosely with aluminum foil. Let rest for 15 minutes.

❀ Arrange the chicken on a warmed platter. Serve with the skimmed pan juices, if desired.

NUTRITIONAL ANALYSIS PER SERVING: Calories 659 (Kilojoules 2,768); Protein 60 g; Carbohydrates 4 g; Total Fat 44 g; Saturated Fat 11 g; Cholesterol 189 mg; Sodium 476 mg; Dietary Fiber 0 g

Seafood Curry with Coconut, Citrus, and Cucumber

PREP TIME: 40 MINUTES

COOKING TIME: 30 MINUTES

INGREDIENTS

2 teaspoons ground coriander

1 teaspoon ground cumin

½ teaspoon ground pepper

3 tablespoons peanut oil

1 yellow onion, finely minced

1 tablespoon each peeled and grated
   fresh ginger and finely minced garlic

2 teaspoons each grated lime zest
   and minced lemongrass

1–2 teaspoons minced jalapeño chile

2 cups (16 fl oz/500 ml) coconut
   milk

1½ cups (12 fl oz/375 ml) fish or
   chicken broth

¼ cup (⅓ oz/10 g) fresh cilantro
   (fresh coriander), puréed with
   1 tablespoon water

1 tablespoon lime juice, or to taste

1 tablespoon brown sugar

salt to taste

2 small squid

2 small cucumbers, peeled, quartered
   lengthwise, seeded, and cut into
   2-inch (5-cm) pieces

1 lb (500 g) firm white fish fillets

24 clams, well scrubbed

8 each medium or large shrimp
   (prawns), peeled and deveined,
   and sea scallops

¼ cup (⅓ oz/10 g) each chopped
   fresh mint and cilantro

This Asian-inspired curry, more sweet than hot, pairs nicely with a medium-bodied Australian Riesling that will balance its sweet, citrus, and hot tones. An off-dry white or rosé picks up on the nuance of the sweet coconut.

DEPENDABLE: DRY, UNOAKED AUSTRALIAN RIESLING
DARING: OFF-DRY MUSCAT SUCH AS ITALIAN MOSCATO D'ASTI

SERVES 4

✽ In a small sauté pan over medium heat, toast the coriander, cumin, and pepper, shaking the pan often, until fragrant, 2–3 minutes; reserve.

✽ In a very large saucepan over medium heat, warm the oil. Add the onion and sauté until translucent, about 5 minutes. Add the ginger, garlic, lime zest, lemongrass, chile, and toasted spices and cook, stirring, until fragrant, 3–4 minutes. Add the coconut milk, broth, puréed cilantro, lime juice, and brown sugar, bring to a boil, and reduce the heat to low immediately. Simmer for 5 minutes to blend the flavors of the curry base. Season with salt and set aside.

✽ Meanwhile, clean the squid: Working with 1 squid at a time, pull the head from the body. Cut the head from the tentacles above the eyes and discard the head. Squeeze the hard "beak" from the base of the tentacles. Cut the tentacles in half and set them aside. Remove the transparent "quill" from the body and discard; rinse the body well and peel off the speckled skin. Cut the body into rings 1 inch (2.5 cm) wide. Set aside.

✽ Bring a saucepan three-fourths full of salted water to a boil. Add the cucumbers, boil for 3 minutes, drain, and cool under running water.

✽ Return the curry base to a simmer over medium heat. Cut the fish into 2-inch (5-cm) cubes and add to the base along with the clams (discarding any that fail to close to the touch) and cucumbers. Simmer until the fish is opaque throughout, 8 minutes. Add the shrimp, scallops, and squid during the last 3 minutes of cooking.

✽ Spoon into a warmed serving bowl, discarding any clams that failed to open. Garnish with the mint and cilantro and serve.

NUTRITIONAL ANALYSIS PER SERVING: Calories 633 (Kilojoules 2,659); Protein 53 g; Carbohydrates 20 g; Total Fat 39 g; Saturated Fat 24 g; Cholesterol 176 mg; Sodium 622 mg; Dietary Fiber 2 g

Linguine with Clams

PREP TIME: 30 MINUTES

COOKING TIME: 20 MINUTES

INGREDIENTS

6 dozen Manila clams or 3–4 dozen
   larger hard-shell clams, 4–5 lb
   (2–2.5 kg) total, well scrubbed

1 cup (8 fl oz/250 ml) dry white wine

1 lb (500 g) dried linguine

½ cup (4 fl oz/125 ml) extra-virgin
   olive oil

4 teaspoons finely minced garlic,
   or to taste

pinch of dried oregano (optional)

pinch of red pepper flakes (optional)

½ cup (¾ oz/20 g) chopped fresh
   flat-leaf (Italian) parsley

ground black pepper to taste

salt to taste

3 tablespoons unsalted butter or
   extra-virgin olive oil (optional)

SERVING TIP: If you leave the clams
in their shells when serving, be sure
to put 1 or more large bowls on the
table into which guests can discard
shells as they eat.

Clams are a bit tricky to partner with wine, especially if they
are briny. The saltier the clam, the greater the need for a zesty,
tart white that performs the same role as a squeeze of lemon
juice—that is, balances the saltiness with acidity. If you're using
sweeter clams, a complex and buttery white wine is appropriate.

DEPENDABLE: GAVI OR OTHER CORTESE-BASED ITALIAN WHITE WINE
DARING: TART, DRY EUROPEAN ROSÉ

SERVES 4

❋ Discard any clams that do not close to the touch. In a large sauté pan,
combine the clams and white wine. Place over high heat, cover, and
steam, shaking the pan occasionally, until the clams open, 3–4 minutes
for Manila clams or 5–7 minutes for larger clams. Using a slotted
spoon, transfer the clams to a shallow bowl. Discard any clams that
failed to open. Line a fine-mesh sieve with cheesecloth (muslin), place
over a bowl, and strain the pan juices. If using small clams, you may
leave them in their shells or remove them, but leave them whole. If the
clams are large, let them cool until they can be handled, then remove
the meats from the shells, capturing any juices. Chop the clams into
bite-sized pieces, place in a bowl, and pour the strained juices over them.
Then, pour any captured juices through the lined sieve held over the
bowl holding the clams.

❋ Bring a large pot three-fourths full of salted water to a boil. Add the
pasta, stir well, and cook until al dente (tender, but still firm to the bite),
about 10 minutes or according to package directions.

❋ Meanwhile, in the same sauté pan over low heat, warm the olive oil.
Add the garlic, oregano (if using), and red pepper flakes (if using) and
sauté until warmed through, 1–2 minutes. Add the clams and their
juices and heat through gently. Do not overcook, or the clams will tough-
en. Add the parsley and a generous amount of black pepper. Season
with salt if the clams are not salty enough, then swirl in the butter or
olive oil, if using.

❋ Drain the linguine and transfer to a warmed serving bowl. Add the
clam sauce and toss well. Serve at once.

NUTRITIONAL ANALYSIS PER SERVING: Calories 841 (Kilojoules 3,532); Protein 25 g;
Carbohydrates 89 g; Total Fat 39 g; Saturated Fat 10 g; Cholesterol 50 mg; Sodium 445 mg;
Dietary Fiber 3 g

Roast Salmon with Melting Onions

PREP TIME: 30 MINUTES

COOKING TIME: 40 MINUTES

INGREDIENTS

FOR THE TOASTED BREAD CRUMBS AND ALMONDS

2 cups (4 oz/125 g) cubed Italian or French bread, without crusts

1 teaspoon salt

1 teaspoon ground pepper

½ cup (4 fl oz/125 ml) olive oil or melted unsalted butter

1 cup (4 oz/125 g) sliced (flaked) almonds

5 tablespoons (2½ oz/75 g) unsalted butter

2 yellow onions, cut into slices ¼ inch (6 mm) thick

1 tablespoon chopped fresh sage

1 tablespoon grated lemon zest

salt and ground pepper to taste

4 salmon fillets, about 6 oz (185 g) each

1 lemon, quartered

MAKE-AHEAD TIP: The dish can be assembled several hours ahead, covered, and refrigerated, and then baked just before serving.

Richly textured salmon, sweet and tender onions, and the oiliness of the almonds call for a fat, smooth white wine to carry the flavors a little longer. The bread crumbs provide an opportunity to play off the toastiness of an oak-aged wine. But make certain the wine does have some acidity, or the combination will taste too rich and flat. Spinach, sautéed fennel, or broccoli makes an ideal accompaniment.

DEPENDABLE: PINOT GRIS FROM OREGON OR ALSACE
DARING: LIGHT SANGIOVESE FROM TUSCANY OR THE UNITED STATES

SERVES 4

❀ Preheat an oven to 350°F (180°C).

❀ To make the toasted bread crumbs, place the bread cubes in a food processor. Pulse until coarse crumbs form. Spread the crumbs on a baking sheet. In a small bowl, stir the salt and pepper into the oil or butter, and drizzle evenly over the bread crumbs. Bake, stirring occasionally to ensure even browning, until golden but not hard, 15–20 minutes. Remove from the oven and pour into a bowl. Spread the almonds on the same baking sheet and toast in the oven until they take on color and are fragrant, 5–8 minutes. Add to the crumbs and toss to mix. Set aside.

❀ Raise the oven temperature to 450°F (230°C).

❀ Meanwhile, in a sauté pan over medium heat, melt 4 tablespoons (2 oz/60 g) of the butter. Add the onions and cook, stirring occasionally, until tender and sweet, 15–20 minutes. Add the sage and lemon zest. Season with salt and pepper. Stir well. Remove from the heat and set aside.

❀ Select a baking dish large enough to hold the salmon fillets. Butter the dish with the remaining 1 tablespoon of butter and place the fillets in the dish. Sprinkle with salt and pepper. Top with the onion mixture, covering evenly, then top with the almond-crumb mixture.

❀ Bake until opaque throughout when pierced with a knife, 8–10 minutes. Transfer the fillets to warmed individual plates and serve immediately with the lemon wedges.

NUTRITIONAL ANALYSIS PER SERVING: Calories 961 (Kilojoules 4,036); Protein 44 g; Carbohydrates 31 g; Total Fat 76 g; Saturated Fat 18 g; Cholesterol 139 mg; Sodium 857 mg; Dietary Fiber 4 g

Crab, Pasta, and Cheese Gratin

PREP TIME: 30 MINUTES

COOKING TIME: 55 MINUTES,
    PLUS 10 MINUTES FOR
    COOLING

INGREDIENTS

¾ lb (375 g) macaroni

1 tablespoon olive oil

1 cup (5 oz/155 g) shelled peas
    (optional)

6 tablespoons (3 oz/90 g) unsalted
    butter

¼ cup (1½ oz/45 g) all-purpose
    (plain) flour

2 cups (16 fl oz/500 ml) milk, heated

½ cup (4 fl oz/125 ml) heavy (double)
    cream, heated

salt and ground pepper to taste

ground nutmeg to taste

⅔ lb (315 g) lump crabmeat, picked
    over for shell fragments

3 tablespoons chopped fresh chives

½ cup (2 oz/60 g) finely shredded
    fontina or Emmentaler cheese

½ cup (2 oz/60 g) plus 3 tablespoons
    grated Parmesan cheese

½ cup (2 oz/60 g) plus 3 tablespoons
    finely shredded white cheddar
    cheese

½ cup (2 oz/60 g) fine dried bread
    crumbs

Mild cheeses marry better with white wines than red wines because of their delicate flavors and the creaminess in both the wine and the food. Add the resonance of sweet crab and a lush Chardonnay is the obvious choice; but other fruity, rich white wines also work well with this classic comfort food.

DEPENDABLE: FULL, FRUITY CHARDONNAY
DARING: FRESH, LIGHT DOLCETTO

SERVES 4

❀ Preheat an oven to 400°F (200°C). Butter a 2-qt (2-l) baking dish.

❀ Bring a large pot three-fourths full of salted water to a boil. Add the macaroni, stir well, and cook until al dente (tender, but firm to the bite), 10–12 minutes. Drain, rinse under cold water to halt the cooking, and drain again. Transfer to a bowl and toss with the olive oil. Set aside.

❀ If using the peas, bring a small saucepan three-fourths full of salted water to a boil. Add the peas and cook until nearly tender, about 3 minutes. Drain, rinse under cold running water to halt the cooking, and drain again. Set aside.

❀ In a saucepan over medium heat, melt 4 tablespoons (2 oz/60 g) of the butter. Add the flour and cook, stirring, until fully incorporated, about 3 minutes; do not allow to brown. Slowly add the milk and cream, whisking constantly. Bring to a boil, reduce the heat to low, and simmer, stirring occasionally, until smooth and thickened, about 5 minutes. Season with salt, pepper, and nutmeg.

❀ Add the sauce to the macaroni and mix well. Fold in the crabmeat, chives, peas (if using), and ½ cup (2 oz/60 g) each of the fontina or Emmentaler, Parmesan, and cheddar cheeses. Transfer to the prepared baking dish. Top with the 3 tablespoons each Parmesan and cheddar, sprinkling evenly over the surface. Then sprinkle with the bread crumbs. Finally, cut the remaining 2 tablespoons butter into bits and use to dot the top of the gratin.

❀ Bake until bubbly and golden brown, 25–30 minutes. Remove from the oven and let stand for 10 minutes, then scoop out with a spoon to serve.

NUTRITIONAL ANALYSIS PER SERVING: Calories 1,067 (Kilojoules 4,481); Protein 49 g; Carbohydrates 90 g; Total Fat 56 g; Saturated Fat 32 g; Cholesterol 233 mg; Sodium 1,261 mg; Dietary Fiber 3 g

Sautéed Scallops with Orange, Fennel, and Ginger

PREP TIME: 20 MINUTES

COOKING TIME: 30 MINUTES

INGREDIENTS

2 fennel bulbs

8 tablespoons (4 oz/125 g) unsalted
butter

1 cup (8 fl oz/250 ml) fish or chicken
broth

2 lb (1 kg) sea scallops

2 shallots, minced

1 tablespoon grated orange zest

1 teaspoon peeled and grated fresh
ginger

1 cup (8 fl oz/250 ml) dry white
wine or dry vermouth

COOKING TIP: For a more delicate
texture, do not sear the scallops.
Instead simply poach them gently
for 2–3 minutes in the wine or vermouth after the ginger is added,
transfer them to a plate, and then
reduce the wine or vermouth.

Scallops are best partnered by a wine with a profile of flavors
that enhances their inherently succulent, sweet nature. Here,
the added nuances of orange, fennel, and ginger contribute a
playful platform of tastes that marry with full-flavored, full-bodied
white wines. Serve with simple roast potatoes or saffron rice.

DEPENDABLE: ROBUST MARSANNE FROM FRANCE OR CALIFORNIA
DARING: RICH BRUT CHAMPAGNE OR SPARKLING WINE

SERVES 4

❋ Cut off the stems and feathery tops and any bruised outer stalks
from the fennel bulbs. Coarsely chop enough of the feathery tops to
yield ¼ cup (⅓ oz/10 g) and set aside. Core the fennel bulbs and thinly
slice crosswise or lengthwise.

❋ In a sauté pan over medium heat, melt 2 tablespoons of the butter.
Add the fennel and sauté, turning often and gradually adding the broth,
until the fennel is tender and most of the broth is absorbed, about 10 minutes. Remove from the heat and set aside.

❋ In a large sauté pan over high heat, melt 2 tablespoons of the butter.
Add the scallops and sear, turning once, until pale gold on both sides,
but still quite soft, 2–3 minutes total. Transfer to a plate.

❋ In the same pan over medium heat, melt 2 tablespoons of the butter.
Add the shallots and sauté until softened, about 5 minutes. Add the
orange zest, ginger, and wine or vermouth and cook until the liquid is
reduced by half, 5–8 minutes. Return the fennel and scallops to the pan
and warm through quickly. Stir in the remaining 2 tablespoons butter.

❋ Transfer to a warmed serving dish and sprinkle with the chopped
fennel fronds. Serve immediately.

NUTRITIONAL ANALYSIS PER SERVING: Calories 444 (Kilojoules 1,865); Protein 41 g;
Carbohydrates 12 g; Total Fat 25 g; Saturated Fat 15 g; Cholesterol 137 mg; Sodium 775 mg;
Dietary Fiber 2 g

Indian Chicken Curry with Coconut and Spiced Onions

PREP TIME: 20 MINUTES

COOKING TIME: 40 MINUTES

INGREDIENTS

2½ lb (1.25 kg) chicken parts
(8–12 pieces)

salt and ground black pepper to
taste

¼ cup (2 fl oz/60 ml) peanut oil

1½–2 cups (6–8 oz/185–250 g)
chopped yellow onion

2 tablespoons peeled and minced
fresh ginger

1 tablespoon minced garlic

½ teaspoon ground cardamom

½ teaspoon ground cinnamon

½ teaspoon ground fennel

½ teaspoon ground turmeric

¼ teaspoon ground cloves

⅛ teaspoon cayenne pepper

1½ cups (12 fl oz/375 ml) coconut
milk

¼ cup (1¼ oz/37 g) slivered blanched
almonds

½ cup (4 fl oz/125 ml) heavy (double)
cream

2 tablespoons chopped fresh
cilantro (fresh coriander) or mint

MAKE-AHEAD TIP: The curry can be
made up to 1 day ahead, covered, and
refrigerated. Reheat over low heat.

A tropical fruit–scented white wine with a somewhat oily texture
beautifully accompanies the silkiness that comes from the coconut
milk and cream in this braised mélange. The bright fruit flavors
of a Viognier are sublime with the sweet and aromatic qualities
of the spices. Round out the menu with spinach sautéed with
ginger and garlic, and basmati rice cooked with a cinnamon stick
and a few whole cloves.

DEPENDABLE: FRESH, FULL VIOGNIER
DARING: OFF-DRY, TART RIESLING

SERVES 4

❊ Rinse the chicken pieces and pat dry with paper towels. Sprinkle with
salt and black pepper and set aside.

❊ In a sauté pan large enough to hold all of the chicken pieces in a
single layer, warm the peanut oil over medium heat. Add the onion,
ginger, and garlic and sauté, stirring from time to time to prevent sticking, until softened, 5–8 minutes. Add the cardamom, cinnamon, fennel,
turmeric, cloves, and cayenne and sauté to blend the spices and release
their aromatic oils, about 2 minutes. Add the chicken pieces and turn
in the onion-spice mixture for about 2 minutes to coat well. Add the
coconut milk and bring to a boil. Reduce the heat to low, cover, and
simmer until the chicken is very tender, about 30 minutes.

❊ Meanwhile, preheat an oven to 350°F (180°C). Spread the almonds on
a baking sheet and toast in the oven until they take on color and are fragrant, 5–8 minutes. Remove from the oven and set aside until needed.

❊ When the chicken is tender, add the almonds and cream and stir to
combine. Season with salt and black pepper.

❊ Transfer to warmed plates and sprinkle with the cilantro or mint.
Serve immediately.

NUTRITIONAL ANALYSIS PER SERVING: Calories 883 (Kilojoules 3,708); Protein 41 g;
Carbohydrates 11 g; Total Fat 76 g; Saturated Fat 34 g; Cholesterol 185 mg; Sodium 161 mg;
Dietary Fiber 2 g

Lobster with Basil Butter

PREP TIME: 30 MINUTES

COOKING TIME: 25 MINUTES

INGREDIENTS

4 lobsters, about 1½ lb (750 g) each

FOR THE BASIL BUTTER

leaves from 1 large bunch fresh basil
(about 1½ cups/1½ oz/45 g leaves)

½ cup (4 oz/125 g) unsalted butter,
at room temperature

salt and ground pepper to taste

lemon juice to taste (optional)

MAKE-AHEAD TIP: Boil the lobsters
as directed, remove from the boiling
water, and immerse in an ice-water
bath to arrest the cooking. Refrigerate
for up to 6 hours before cleaning
and baking the lobsters.

If ever a food were put on earth for a specific wine, lobsters were made for Chardonnay. Broiled, grilled, baked, or steamed, their subtle sweetness and soft texture magnificently mirror the wine's lushness.

DEPENDABLE: LUSH, LIGHTLY OAK-AGED CHARDONNAY
DARING: PINOT NOIR FROM THE UNITED STATES

SERVES 4

❈ Bring a large pot three-fourths full of salted water to a rolling boil. Drop in the lobsters and, after the water returns to a boil, reduce the heat to medium-low. Simmer until almost cooked, 7–8 minutes. Using tongs, remove the lobsters. When cool enough to handle, lay them on a work surface. Working with 1 lobster at a time, insert the tip of a sharp knife into the point where the tail and body sections meet and cut through the tail. Turn the lobster around and continue to cut from the center through the head, cutting in half. Discard the green-black vein that runs the length of the body meat, as well as the small sand sac at the base of the head. If desired, reserve the green tomalley ("lobster butter") and any coral roe for using in the basil butter. Grip the fins of a tail half with one hand and pull out the tail meat in a single piece. Repeat with the other tail half. Set the meat aside. Twist off the claws from the body shell. Crack the claws and remove all the claw and knuckle meat. Cut the tail meat into 1-inch (2.5-cm) segments and put it back into the tail shells along with the claw and knuckle meat.

❈ Preheat an oven to 350°F (180°C).

❈ To make the basil butter, bring a saucepan three-fourths full of water to a boil. Add the basil leaves and blanch for 15 seconds. Drain, refresh in ice water, and drain again. Dry well with paper towels. In a blender or food processor, combine the basil, butter, and the tomalley and roe, if using. Process until well incorporated. Season with salt and pepper and with lemon juice, if using.

❈ Spread the basil butter on the lobster meat, covering evenly. Cover loosely with aluminum foil and bake until tender, 10–15 minutes. (The basil butter will darken, but the taste will still be good.) Remove from the oven, transfer to individual plates, and serve.

NUTRITIONAL ANALYSIS PER SERVING: Calories 353 (Kilojoules 1,482); Protein 31 g; Carbohydrates 2 g; Total Fat 24 g; Saturated Fat 14 g; Cholesterol 170 mg; Sodium 573 mg; Dietary Fiber 0 g

Salmon Poached in Red Wine

PREP TIME: 10 MINUTES

COOKING TIME: 25 MINUTES

INGREDIENTS

4 salmon fillets, about 6 oz (185 g) each

salt and ground pepper to taste

2–3 cups (16–24 fl oz/500–750 ml) light red wine

¼ cup (⅓ oz/10 g) chopped fresh tarragon

¼ cup (2 oz/60 g) unsalted butter, at room temperature, cut into slivers

A medium- to full-bodied white wine can be delicious with poached salmon, but a light-bodied red wine is better when the poaching liquid and the sauce are based on red wine. Avoid reds with a lot of tannins, which would be too astringent for a nonoily fish. Serve the salmon with mashed potatoes and green beans, asparagus, or sautéed spinach.

DEPENDABLE: LIGHTLY OAKED PINOT NOIR
DARING: FRESH SÉMILLON BLEND

SERVES 4

❊ Sprinkle the salmon fillets with salt and pepper.

❊ In a sauté pan wide enough to accommodate all the salmon fillets in a single layer, pour in the wine to a depth of 1½–2 inches (4–5 cm). Bring to a boil over high heat. Slip in the salmon fillets, reduce the heat to low so the wine is at a bare simmer, cover, and cook until the salmon is opaque throughout when pierced with a knife, 8–10 minutes. If the fillets are not completely covered by the wine, turn them once at the midpoint so they will take on a uniformly red color. Using a slotted spatula, transfer the salmon to a warmed platter or individual plates and keep warm.

❊ Raise the heat to high, bring the poaching liquid to a boil, and boil until reduced to about ½ cup (4 fl oz/125 ml), about 15 minutes, adding the tarragon at the midpoint. The pan juices will be thickened and slightly syrupy. Remove from the heat and swirl in the butter.

❊ Pour the sauce under or over the salmon. Serve at once.

NUTRITIONAL ANALYSIS PER SERVING: Calories 428 (Kilojoules 1,977); Protein 35 g; Carbohydrates 3 g; Total Fat 30 g; Saturated Fat 11 g; Cholesterol 131 mg; Sodium 110 mg; Dietary Fiber 0 g

Lamb Chops with Moroccan Spices

PREP TIME: 10 MINUTES, PLUS
2 HOURS FOR MARINATING

COOKING TIME: 10 MINUTES,
PLUS PREPARING FIRE

INGREDIENTS

½ cup (¾ oz/20 g) chopped fresh
mint, plus extra for garnish
(optional)

1 tablespoon ground coriander

2 teaspoons finely minced garlic

1 teaspoon sweet paprika

1 teaspoon ground cumin

1 teaspoon ground black pepper

¼ teaspoon cayenne pepper

salt to taste

juice of 1 lemon

2 tablespoons olive oil

8 loin lamb chops or 16 small rib
chops

While lamb and Pinot Noir are commonly paired, this prepara-tion of lamb, with its use of earthy, pungent, hot, and sweet spices, tastes best with a more assertive red. Ample tannins and some body, in the form of alcohol, are needed to handle the smoky, charred effects of grilling. Serve the chops with couscous and sautéed beets and carrots glazed with butter, orange juice and zest, and a hint of mint.

DEPENDABLE: SPICY SYRAH BLEND OR ZINFANDEL
DARING: CALIFORNIAN OR AUSTRALIAN GRENACHE-BASED ROSÉ

SERVES 4

❀ In a small bowl, stir together the ½ cup (¾ oz/20 g) mint, the corian-der, garlic, paprika, cumin, black pepper, cayenne pepper, salt, lemon juice, and olive oil. Rub the mixture into the chops, coating evenly, and place in a nonaluminum container. Cover and marinate at cool room temperature for 2 hours or for up to overnight in the refrigerator.

❀ Prepare a fire in a charcoal grill. If the chops are refrigerated, bring to room temperature.

❀ Place the chops on an oiled grill rack and grill, turning once, for 4 minutes on each side for medium-rare, or until done to your liking.

❀ Transfer to a warmed platter or individual plates and sprinkle with mint, if using. Serve at once.

NUTRITIONAL ANALYSIS PER SERVING: Calories 499 (Kilojoules 2,096); Protein 35 g; Carbohydrates 3 g; Total Fat 38 g; Saturated Fat 14 g; Cholesterol 135 mg; Sodium 108 mg; Dietary Fiber 1 g

Cornish Hens with Grapes and Sage

PREP TIME: 20 MINUTES

COOKING TIME: 1 HOUR

INGREDIENTS

4 Cornish hens or poussins, about
   1 lb (500 g) each, or 8 boneless
   quail

salt and ground pepper to taste

24 fresh sage leaves, plus 2 tablespoons chopped

2 tablespoons unsalted butter

2 tablespoons olive oil

2 cups (12 oz/375 g) red or black
   seedless grapes, plus 1 cup (6 oz/
   185 g), halved

1 cup (8 fl oz/250 ml) rich chicken
   broth

Cornish hens, like quail and poussins, are mildly flavored poultry and flexible in terms of compatible wines. Look for predominant flavors in the stuffing or sauce. Here, the dark grapes and sage steer you toward a light- to medium-bodied red wine. Serve with a simple risotto or polenta.

DEPENDABLE: CORVINA (VALPOLICELLA) FROM NORTHERN ITALY
DARING: PEPPERY ROSÉ FROM PROVENCE OR RHÔNE VALLEY

SERVES 4

❀ Rinse the birds and pat dry with paper towels. Sprinkle inside and out with salt and pepper.

❀ Using your fingers, carefully loosen the breast skin on each bird. Tuck 4 sage leaves under the skin of each Cornish hen or poussin, or 2 leaves under the skin of each quail, positioning them evenly over the breasts. Pat the skin firmly back in place. Tuck 2 sage leaves inside the cavity of each Cornish hen or poussin, or 1 leaf inside each quail.

❀ Preheat an oven to 350°F (180°C).

❀ In a large sauté pan over medium-high heat, melt the butter with the olive oil. Add the birds and cook, turning often, until well browned on all sides, 10–15 minutes. Transfer the birds to a roasting pan and place in the oven. Roast until done and the juices run clear when a leg is pierced with a knife, 35–45 minutes for Cornish hens or poussins, or 10–15 minutes for the quail.

❀ While the birds are roasting, in a blender or food processor, process the 2 cups (12 oz/375 g) grapes until puréed. Pour the chicken broth into a small saucepan and place over high heat. Bring to a boil and boil until reduced by half, 8–10 minutes. Add the puréed grapes and chopped sage, reduce the heat to medium, and simmer until slightly thickened, about 5 minutes. Add the halved grapes and heat until warmed through.

❀ Transfer the birds to warmed individual plates. (If desired, cut the Cornish hens or poussins in half with poultry shears.) Spoon the sauce over the birds and serve at once.

NUTRITIONAL ANALYSIS PER SERVING: Calories 706 (Kilojoules 2,965); Protein 44 g; Carbohydrates 23 g; Total Fat 49 g; Saturated Fat 14 g; Cholesterol 265 mg; Sodium 375 mg; Dietary Fiber 2 g

Sautéed Veal with Prosciutto and Sage

PREP TIME: 10 MINUTES

COOKING TIME: 20 MINUTES

INGREDIENTS

1½ lb (750 g) veal scallops (about 8 total), each ⅓–½ inch (9–12 mm) thick

salt and ground pepper to taste

16 fresh sage leaves

8 thin slices prosciutto

3 tablespoons olive oil

½ cup (4 fl oz/125 ml) beef, veal, or rich chicken broth

½ cup (4 fl oz/125 ml) dry Marsala

¼ cup (2 oz/60 g) unsalted butter, at room temperature, cut into slivers

PREP TIP: This dish may be prepared with boneless chicken or turkey breasts as well.

The mildness of veal in this recipe is the least significant issue for the wine. The prosciutto and sage are relatively strong, suggesting a red wine. Because salt amplifies the perception of alcohol, choose a light- to medium-bodied red. A wine with a little more oak for the perception of oak sweetness will balance the Marsala used for deglazing the pan. Serve with asparagus or green beans and mashed potatoes.

DEPENDABLE: SANGIOVESE BLEND FROM ITALY
DARING: FRESH, CRISP ITALIAN WHITE SUCH AS FRASCATI OR ORVIETO

SERVES 4

❀ One at a time, place the veal scallops between 2 sheets of plastic wrap and gently pound with a meat pounder until about ¼ inch (6 mm) thick.

❀ Sprinkle the veal lightly with salt and pepper, and top each piece with 2 sage leaves. Cover the sage leaves on each scallop with 1 slice prosciutto and secure in place with toothpicks.

❀ In a sauté pan large enough to accommodate all the veal slices in a single layer (or using 2 pans), warm the olive oil over medium-high heat. Add the veal scallops and sauté until golden, about 3 minutes. Turn and sauté the second side until golden, 3–4 minutes longer. Transfer the veal to a warmed platter or individual plates, remove the toothpicks, and keep warm.

❀ Return the pan to high heat. Pour in the broth and Marsala and deglaze the pan, stirring with a wooden spoon to remove any browned bits from the pan bottom. Reduce the pan juices until thickened, 8–10 minutes. Remove from the heat and swirl in the butter.

❀ Spoon the pan juices over the veal and serve at once.

NUTRITIONAL ANALYSIS PER SERVING: Calories 496 (Kilojoules 2,083); Protein 44 g; Carbohydrates 1 g; Total Fat 31 g; Saturated Fat 12 g; Cholesterol 187 mg; Sodium 738 mg; Dietary Fiber 0 g

Pasta with Tomatoes and Eggplant

PREP TIME: 20 MINUTES,
PLUS 30 MINUTES FOR
DRAINING EGGPLANT

COOKING TIME: 25 MINUTES

INGREDIENTS

1 eggplant (aubergine), about 1 lb (500 g), peeled and cut into 1-inch (2.5-cm) pieces

salt

6 tablespoons (3 fl oz/90 ml) extra-virgin olive oil, or as needed

6–8 green (spring) onions, including tender green tops, chopped

1½ tablespoons finely minced garlic

½–1 teaspoon red pepper flakes

½ cup (4 fl oz/125 ml) dry white wine

1½ cups (9 oz/280 g) peeled, seeded, and chopped plum (Roma) tomatoes (fresh or canned)

ground black pepper to taste

3 tablespoons chopped fresh mint, basil, marjoram, or flat-leaf (Italian) parsley

1 lb (500 g) penne, rigatoni, or other dried short pasta

½ cup (2 oz/60 g) grated ricotta salata cheese, plus extra for passing (optional)

In a lesson from the "old school" of wine and food pairing, the red sauce here calls for a red wine. The wine needs sufficient acidity for the tomatoes (tomatoes are tart by nature) and enough tannins to hold up against the slight bitterness in the eggplants. A Chianti or other Sangiovese-based wine performs deliciously.

DEPENDABLE: SANGIOVESE BLEND
DARING: LIGHTLY OAK-AGED WHITE SUCH AS A SOAVE

SERVES 4

❀ Sprinkle the eggplant pieces with salt and place in a colander. Let stand for 30 minutes to drain off the bitter juices. Rinse and pat dry with paper towels. Set aside.

❀ In a large sauté pan over medium heat, warm 2 tablespoons of the olive oil. Add the green onions and sauté until softened, about 3 minutes. Add the garlic and red pepper flakes and sauté until fragrant, about 1 minute. Add the white wine and let it bubble up and almost evaporate, about 3 minutes. Add the tomatoes and simmer, crushing the tomatoes with a wooden spoon, until the sauce thickens slightly, about 5 minutes. Season with salt and black pepper. Stir in 2 tablespoons of the chopped herbs and keep warm.

❀ Bring a large pot three-fourths full of salted water to a boil. Drop in the pasta, stir well, and cook until al dente (tender, but firm to the bite), 10–12 minutes or according to package directions.

❀ Meanwhile, in another sauté pan over high heat, warm the remaining 4 tablespoons (2 fl oz/60 ml) olive oil. Add the eggplant and sauté until golden, about 8 minutes, adding more oil as needed to prevent scorching. Add the eggplant to the tomato sauce and simmer for a few minutes to heat through.

❀ Drain the pasta and place in a warmed serving bowl. Add the sauce and toss well. Sprinkle with the cheese and the remaining 1 tablespoon chopped herbs. Serve at once. Pass more cheese at the table, if you like.

NUTRITIONAL ANALYSIS PER SERVING: Calories 702 (Kilojoules 2,948); Protein 19 g; Carbohydrates 100 g; Total Fat 26 g; Saturated Fat 5 g; Cholesterol 13 mg; Sodium 654 mg; Dietary Fiber 6 g

Grilled Tuna with Sun-Dried Tomatoes and Olives

PREP TIME: 20 MINUTES

COOKING TIME: 6 MINUTES,
   PLUS PREPARING FIRE

INGREDIENTS

¼ cup (2 oz/60 g) finely chopped
   oil-packed sun-dried tomatoes

¼ cup (1¼ oz/37 g) chopped pitted
   Gaeta or Niçoise olives

¼ cup (⅓ oz/10 g) chopped fresh
   mint or thyme

2 teaspoons minced garlic

4 tablespoons (2 fl oz/60 ml) extra-
   virgin olive oil

3 tablespoons lemon juice

2 tablespoons oil from sun-dried
   tomatoes

½ teaspoon ground pepper, plus
   pepper to taste

4 tuna fillets, 6–7 oz (185–220 g)
   each

salt to taste

COOKING TIP: Take care not to overcook the fish. Tuna, despite its simi-
larity to steak, dries out faster.

Close your eyes, bite into a piece of seared tuna, and you just might think of filet mignon. Tuna has a meaty texture and doesn't taste very fishy, so drink what you would want with steak. The sun-dried tomatoes and pungent olives pair superbly with a medium-bodied red wine. Serve the tuna with roast potatoes and sautéed greens like Swiss chard or escarole (Batavian endive). Grilled eggplant (aubergine) and zucchini (courgettes) are also fine accompaniments.

DEPENDABLE: SOFT, LIGHTLY OAK-AGED MERLOT
DARING: FRAGRANT, SPICY ROSÉ BLEND

SERVES 4

❊ Prepare a fire in a charcoal grill or preheat a broiler (griller).

❊ In a bowl, stir together the sun-dried tomatoes, olives, mint or thyme, garlic, 3 tablespoons of the olive oil, lemon juice, oil from the tomatoes, and ½ teaspoon pepper.

❊ Brush the remaining 1 tablespoon olive oil evenly over both sides of the fish fillets. Sprinkle the fillets with salt and pepper.

❊ Place the fish on the grill rack, or place on a rack in a broiler pan and slip under the broiler. Grill or broil, turning once, for 3 minutes on each side for medium-rare, or until done to your liking.

❊ Transfer the fish fillets to warmed individual plates and spoon an equal amount of the sauce over each serving. Serve immediately.

NUTRITIONAL ANALYSIS PER SERVING: Calories 460 (Kilojoules 1,932); Protein 45 g; Carbohydrates 8 g; Total Fat 28 g; Saturated Fat 4 g; Cholesterol 83 mg; Sodium 440 mg; Dietary Fiber 2 g

Polenta with Mushrooms and Cheese

PREP TIME: 20 MINUTES,
  PLUS 1 HOUR FOR SOAKING
  PORCINI, IF USING

COOKING TIME: 50 MINUTES

INGREDIENTS

FOR THE MUSHROOM SAUCE

1 oz (30 g) dried porcini mushrooms (optional)

about ⅓ cup (3 fl oz/80 ml) hot water, if using dried mushrooms

4 tablespoons (2 fl oz/60 ml) olive oil

1 yellow onion, chopped

3 tablespoons unsalted butter

1 lb (500 g) assorted fresh mushrooms such as cremini, portobello, chanterelle, and domestic brown or white, in any combination, brushed clean, trimmed, and sliced ¼ inch (6 mm) thick

1 tablespoon minced garlic

1 tablespoon chopped fresh sage or thyme

salt and ground pepper to taste

FOR THE POLENTA

1 cup (5 oz/155 g) coarse cornmeal

1 teaspoon salt, plus salt to taste

4 cups (32 fl oz/1 l) water

3–4 tablespoons (1½–2 oz/45–60 g) unsalted butter

½ cup (4 oz/125 g) mascarpone cheese

⅓ cup (1½ oz/45 g) shredded Parmesan cheese

Merlot's inherent truffle fragrance and earthiness make it an ideal wine for mushrooms. The polenta adds a note of sweetness, which suggests a fruity wine, and it definitely lends bulk to the dish, so pick a Merlot with body. If you use mostly wild mushrooms, an even heftier red wine is not out of the question.

DEPENDABLE: MERLOT FROM FRANCE, ITALY, OR THE UNITED STATES
DARING: MEDIUM-BODIED NEBBIOLO FROM ITALY

SERVES 4

✽ First, make the sauce: If using dried porcini, place in a bowl with the hot water to cover, and let soak until softened, about 1 hour. Remove the porcini, squeezing out the excess water, and chop finely. Line a small sieve with cheesecloth (muslin), place over a small bowl, and pour the liquid through it. Set the mushrooms and liquid aside separately.

✽ In a large sauté pan over medium heat, warm 2 tablespoons of the olive oil. Add the onion and sauté, stirring occasionally, until tender, 8–10 minutes. Remove from the pan and set aside. In the same sauté pan over high heat, warm the remaining 2 tablespoons oil with the butter. Add the fresh mushrooms and sauté until softened, about 8 minutes. Return the onion to the pan and stir in the garlic and sage or thyme. Sauté until fragrant, about 1 minute. Add the chopped dried mushrooms and the soaking liquid, if using, and cook, stirring, for 2 minutes to blend the flavors. Season with salt and pepper. Remove from the heat and keep warm while you cook the polenta.

✽ To make the polenta, in a heavy saucepan over medium heat, combine the cornmeal, the 1 teaspoon salt, and the water. Bring to a simmer, stirring often, and then cook, stirring and scraping the bottom of the pan often, until thick and smooth, about 30 minutes. If the polenta thickens too quickly but still feels undercooked and grainy, stir in a little hot water and keep stirring over medium heat until cooked through and soft. Season to taste with salt and stir in the butter and the mascarpone cheese.

✽ To serve, reheat the mushroom sauce. Spoon the polenta onto a warmed serving platter or individual plates. Top with the mushroom sauce and sprinkle with the Parmesan. Serve at once.

NUTRITIONAL ANALYSIS PER SERVING: Calories 627 (Kilojoules 2,633); Protein 12 g; Carbohydrates 39 g; Total Fat 48 g; Saturated Fat 24 g; Cholesterol 81 mg; Sodium 777 mg; Dietary Fiber 4 g

Roast Pork Loin in Ginger Marinade

PREP TIME: 15 MINUTES, PLUS
6 HOURS FOR MARINATING

COOKING TIME: 1 HOUR, PLUS
10 MINUTES FOR RESTING

INGREDIENTS

3 green (spring) onions, including
tender green tops, chopped

1 piece fresh ginger, 3 inches (7.5 cm)
long, peeled and sliced across the
grain

2 cloves garlic

½ cup (4 fl oz/125 ml) chicken or
beef broth

3 tablespoons soy sauce

2 tablespoons tomato sauce or
tomato ketchup

¼ cup (2 oz/60 g) firmly packed
brown sugar

small pinch of red pepper flakes

1 boneless pork loin, 2½ lb (1.25 kg),
trimmed of all fat

SERVING TIP: The pork is also delicious served at room temperature,
so keep it in mind for picnics or
buffet suppers.

An oak-aged wine complements this roast pork loin because the toasted flavors the barrels impart echo some of the flavors in the caramelized crust. A medium-bodied red with pronounced fruitiness offsets the sweet heat created by the brown sugar, ginger, and soy sauce. Serve with rice and spinach with garlic and sesame seeds.

DEPENDABLE: YOUNG RIOJA OR OTHER OAK-AGED TEMPRANILLO
DARING: OFF-DRY CHENIN BLANC

SERVES 4

❀ In a food processor or blender, combine the green onions, ginger, garlic, chicken or beef broth, soy sauce, tomato sauce or ketchup, brown sugar, and red pepper flakes. Purée to form a marinade. Place the pork loin in a nonaluminum container and pour the marinade over the top. Turn to coat well, then cover and refrigerate for at least 6 hours or for up to overnight.

❀ Bring the pork to room temperature. Preheat an oven to 350°F (180°C).

❀ Transfer the pork loin to a roasting pan. Reserve the marinade. Roast, basting occasionally with the reserved marinade, until an instant-read thermometer inserted into the thickest part of the loin registers 147°–150°F (64°–65°C) or the meat is pale pink when cut in the thickest portion, about 1 hour.

❀ Transfer the pork to a cutting board and cover loosely with aluminum foil. Let rest for 10 minutes.

❀ Slice the pork thinly and arrange the slices on a warmed platter. Serve immediately.

NUTRITIONAL ANALYSIS PER SERVING: Calories 481 (Kilojoules 2,020); Protein 62 g; Carbohydrates 18 g; Total Fat 16 g; Saturated Fat 6 g; Cholesterol 167 mg; Sodium 1,098 mg; Dietary Fiber 1 g

Coq au Vin

PREP TIME: 40 MINUTES

COOKING TIME: 1 HOUR

INGREDIENTS

2 small chickens, 2–2½ lb (1–1.25 kg) each

½ cup (2½ oz/75 g) all-purpose (plain) flour

salt and ground pepper to taste

ground nutmeg to taste

6 tablespoons (3 oz/90 g) unsalted butter

4 tablespoons (2 fl oz/60 ml) olive oil

3 tablespoons brandy, warmed

2 cups (16 fl oz/500 ml) dry red wine

2 cloves garlic

2 fresh thyme sprigs

1 bay leaf

24 fresh cremini or white button mushrooms, brushed clean and stem ends trimmed

16 pearl onions

2 teaspoons sugar

3–4 tablespoons chopped fresh flat-leaf (Italian) parsley

MAKE-AHEAD TIP: The dish can be made up to 2 days in advance and gently reheated just before serving.

This Burgundian classic of chicken simmered in red wine naturally pairs with the wine you use in the cooking.

DEPENDABLE: PINOT NOIR FROM JUST ABOUT ANYWHERE
DARING: A WELL-AGED CABERNET SAUVIGNON

SERVES 4

❀ Working with 1 chicken at a time, lay the bird, breast down, on a work surface. Using poultry shears, cut along both sides of the backbone. Remove the backbone and cut the chicken into quarters. Rinse and pat dry. Spread the flour on a plate and season with salt, pepper, and nutmeg. Dip the chicken pieces in the seasoned flour, shaking off the excess. Set aside.

❀ In a large frying pan over high heat, warm 2 tablespoons each of the butter and olive oil. Add the chicken pieces in batches and brown on all sides, about 15 minutes. As the pieces are browned, transfer them to a heavy pot. When all the pieces have been browned, pour the brandy over them and ignite with a long match. Let the flame die out, then add the wine, garlic, thyme, and bay leaf. Bring to a boil, cover, reduce the heat to low, and simmer until opaque throughout, about 45 minutes.

❀ Meanwhile, in a sauté pan over high heat, warm 2 tablespoons of the butter and the remaining 2 tablespoons oil. Add the mushrooms and sauté until golden, 6–8 minutes. Transfer to a plate and rinse out the pan.

❀ Bring a saucepan three-fourths full of water to a boil. Add the pearl onions and boil for 2–3 minutes. Drain, cut off the root ends, and slip off the skins. Cut a shallow cross in the root ends. Return the onions to the saucepan, add water just to cover, and bring to a boil. Reduce the heat to low, cover partially, and cook until tender but firm, 10–15 minutes. Drain well. In the rinsed sauté pan over high heat, warm the remaining 2 tablespoons butter. Add the onions and sugar and sauté until lightly caramelized, 4–5 minutes. Remove from the heat.

❀ About 10 minutes before the chicken is done, add the mushrooms and onions to the pan and continue cooking as directed. Taste and adjust the seasonings. Transfer to a warmed platter, sprinkle with the parsley, and serve.

NUTRITIONAL ANALYSIS PER SERVING: Calories 1,144 (Kilojoules 4,805); Protein 70 g; Carbohydrates 27 g; Total Fat 84 g; Saturated Fat 28 g; Cholesterol 307 mg; Sodium 261 mg; Dietary Fiber 2 g

Spicy Grilled Ribs

PREP TIME: 30 MINUTES

COOKING TIME: 1½ HOURS,
    PLUS PREPARING FIRE

INGREDIENTS

2 racks baby back ribs, about 4 lb
    (2 kg) total weight

2–3 tablespoons chili powder

salt and ground pepper to taste

FOR THE SAUCE

1 cup (8 fl oz/250 ml) tomato
    ketchup

⅓ cup (3 fl oz/80 ml) cider vinegar

¼ cup (2 fl oz/60 ml) orange juice

⅓ cup (3 oz/90 g) firmly packed
    brown sugar or ½ cup (6 oz/185 g)
    honey

4 cloves garlic, minced

2 tablespoons Worcestershire sauce

2 tablespoons chili powder

1 tablespoon dry mustard

2 teaspoons ground cumin

½ teaspoon ground ginger

¼ teaspoon ground cinnamon

Most people consider ribs to be beer food. But a flavorful, spicy red wine laced with dark fruit flavors mirrors the personality of the sauce in this dish. Some Zinfandels aged in new oak barrels taste a little smoky in their finish—perfect for the grill. For an all-American barbecue, serve with coleslaw and corn bread. For a more Latin touch, serve with black beans and corn on the cob rubbed with chile powder and lime.

DEPENDABLE: ZINFANDEL FROM THE UNITED STATES
DARING: BALANCED WHITE ZINFANDEL OR OTHER OFF-DRY ROSÉ

SERVES 4

❀ Preheat an oven to 350°F (180°C).

❀ Rub the ribs evenly with the chili powder, salt, and pepper. Place on a rack in a roasting pan and cover loosely with aluminum foil. Bake until very tender, about 1 hour.

❀ Meanwhile, make the sauce: In a saucepan, stir together the ketchup, vinegar, orange juice, brown sugar or honey, garlic, Worcestershire sauce, chili powder, mustard, cumin, ginger, and cinnamon. Place over medium heat and bring to a simmer. Cook uncovered, stirring occasionally, until the flavors are well blended, about 15 minutes. Remove from the heat and set aside.

❀ Prepare a fire in a charcoal grill or preheat a broiler (griller).

❀ Sprinkle the ribs lightly with salt and pepper and place on the oiled grill rack or on an oiled rack in a broiler pan. Brush liberally with some of the sauce. Grill or broil until caramelized, 8–10 minutes. Turn, brush with additional sauce, and cook on the second side until crusty and caramelized, about 8 minutes longer.

❀ Transfer to a cutting board and cut the ribs apart. Arrange on a warmed platter and serve. Pour the remaining sauce into a small bowl and pass at the table.

NUTRITIONAL ANALYSIS PER SERVING: Calories 1,012 (Kilojoules 4,250); Protein 56 g; Carbohydrates 48 g; Total Fat 67 g; Saturated Fat 24 g; Cholesterol 258 mg; Sodium 1,112 mg; Dietary Fiber 4 g

Pappardelle with Rich Meat Sauce

PREP TIME: 30 MINUTES, PLUS
1 HOUR FOR SOAKING
PORCINI, IF USING

COOKING TIME: 2½ HOURS

INGREDIENTS

2 oz (60 g) dried porcini mushrooms (optional)

about 1½ cups (12 fl oz/375 ml) hot water, if using dried mushrooms

2 tablespoons unsalted butter

2 tablespoons olive oil

1½ cups (7½ oz/235 g) finely chopped yellow or red (Spanish) onion

⅔ cup (3½ oz/105 g) peeled and finely chopped carrot

½ cup (2½ oz/75 g) finely chopped celery

1 lb (500 g) ground (minced) beef or half beef and half pork

1 cup (8 fl oz/250 ml) white wine

3 tablespoons tomato paste

1 teaspoon salt

1 teaspoon ground pepper

½ teaspoon ground nutmeg

4 cups (32 fl oz/1 l) beef broth, heated

1–2 cups (8–16 fl oz/250–500 ml) heavy (double) cream or milk (optional)

1 lb (500 g) fresh pappardelle

4 tablespoons (2 oz/60 g) unsalted butter (optional)

about ¼ cup (1 oz/30 g) shredded Parmesan cheese

This rich, robust meat sauce is elegantly rustic. Add the pappardelle and the comfort factor is accentuated. The dish calls for a full-bodied, full-flavored red wine. Hearty Italian reds are especially sublime, but you'll have equal success with their counterparts from Spain or France or even muscular reds from the United States. Narrow lasagne noodles or wide fettuccine can be used in place of the pappardelle.

DEPENDABLE: NEBBIOLO BLEND FROM NORTHWESTERN ITALY
DARING: BOLD, DRY ROSÉ FROM FRANCE, CALIFORNIA, OR AUSTRALIA

SERVES 4

❀ If using dried porcini, place in a bowl, add the hot water to cover, and let soak until softened, about 1 hour. Remove the porcini, squeezing out the excess water, and chop finely. Line a small sieve with cheesecloth (muslin), place over a bowl, and pour the soaking liquid through it. Set the mushrooms and liquid aside separately.

❀ In a large sauté pan over medium heat, melt the butter with the oil. Add the onion, carrot, and celery and sauté until lightly colored, about 15 minutes. Add the meat and cook, stirring often, until browned, about 10 minutes. Add the wine and cook until evaporated, 8–10 minutes. Stir in the tomato paste, then add the salt, pepper, nutmeg, broth, and the porcini and strained soaking liquid, if using. Bring to a boil, cover partially, reduce the heat to low, and simmer gently, stirring from time to time, until the flavors are fully blended, about 2 hours.

❀ Taste and adjust the seasonings. If desired, add the cream or milk to round out the flavor, pouring it in slowly until the sauce has a pleasant richness.

❀ Just before serving, bring a large pot three-fourths full of salted water to a boil. Add the pappardelle, stir well, and cook until al dente (tender, but firm to the bite), 2–3 minutes. Drain and transfer to a warmed bowl.

❀ Add the sauce to the pasta and toss well. Divide among warmed individual plates. If you have not added the cream or milk, you can top each portion with 1 tablespoon of the butter, if desired. Pass the Parmesan cheese at the table.

NUTRITIONAL ANALYSIS PER SERVING: Calories 886 (Kilojoules 3,721); Protein 38 g; Carbohydrates 74 g; Total Fat 48 g; Saturated Fat 19 g; Cholesterol 203 mg; Sodium 2,137 mg; Dietary Fiber 5 g

Grilled Peppery Rib-Eye Steak with Roquefort Butter

PREP TIME: 15 MINUTES, PLUS
1 HOUR FOR MARINATING

COOKING TIME: 10 MINUTES,
PLUS PREPARING FIRE

INGREDIENTS

FOR THE ROQUEFORT BUTTER

2 oz (60 g) Roquefort, Gorgonzola,
or other blue-veined cheese

¼ cup (2 oz/60 g) unsalted butter,
at room temperature

1–2 tablespoons cognac (optional)

½ teaspoon ground pepper

2 teaspoons finely minced garlic

1½ teaspoons coarsely ground pepper

2 tablespoons olive oil

4 well-marbled rib-eye, porter-
house, or New York strip steaks,
each 8–10 oz (250–315 g) and
1 inch (2.5 cm) thick

Have you been looking for the perfect occasion to show off
your best Cabernet Sauvignon or classified red Bordeaux? Here
is the ultimate main course for Cabernet-based wines for two
reasons: their tannin magnificently cuts the fat marbled throughout steak, and the flavors are an ideal match. Roquefort cheese
steers you toward France and Bordeaux, but any Cabernet will
be great. Serve with fried or mashed potatoes and a salad of
sliced tomatoes and red onions.

DEPENDABLE: FULL-BODIED CABERNET SAUVIGNON
DARING: ITALIAN SANGIOVESE/CABERNET SAUVIGNON BLEND

SERVES 4

❀ To make the Roquefort butter, in a small food processor, combine
the cheese, butter, cognac to taste (if using), and the ½ teaspoon pepper.
Process to combine thoroughly. Remove from the processor, shape into
a log, and wrap in plastic wrap. Refrigerate until needed. Bring to room
temperature before serving.

❀ In a small bowl, stir together the garlic, coarsely ground pepper, and
enough olive oil to form a thick paste. Place the steaks in a nonaluminum
container and rub the paste evenly into both sides of the steaks. Let stand
at room temperature for at least 1 hour or refrigerate for up to 6 hours.
If refrigerated, bring to room temperature before grilling.

❀ Prepare a fire in a charcoal grill or preheat a broiler (griller).

❀ Place the steaks on the grill rack, or place on a rack in a broiler pan
and slip under the broiler. Grill or broil, turning once, for 3–4 minutes
on each side for medium-rare, or until done to your liking.

❀ Transfer the steaks to warmed individual plates. Cut the Roquefort
butter into equal pieces and place a piece on each steak. Serve immediately.

NUTRITIONAL ANALYSIS PER SERVING: Calories 800 (Kilojoules 3,360); Protein 51 g;
Carbohydrates 2 g; Total Fat 65 g; Saturated Fat 28 g; Cholesterol 201 mg; Sodium 380 mg;
Dietary Fiber 0 g

Hearty Beef Stew

PREP TIME: 30 MINUTES, PLUS
24 HOURS FOR MARINATING

COOKING TIME: 4 HOURS

INGREDIENTS

FOR THE MARINADE

4 cloves garlic, crushed

3 fresh parsley sprigs

3 fresh thyme springs

2 orange zest strips, each 3 inches (7.5 cm) long

12 peppercorns

12 whole cloves

2 allspice berries

1 cinnamon stick

1 bottle (24 fl oz/750 ml) dry red wine

¼ cup (2 fl oz/60 ml) olive oil

2 yellow onions, coarsely chopped

2½ lb (1.25 kg) boneless stewing beef, cut into 2-inch (5-cm) cubes

4 tablespoons (2 fl oz/60 ml) olive oil

2 cups (12 oz/375 g) peeled, seeded, and chopped tomatoes (fresh or canned)

¾ lb (375 g) carrots, peeled and cut into 2-inch (5-cm) lengths

⅔ cup (3½ oz/105 g) brine-cured black olives, pitted if desired

salt and ground pepper to taste

2 tablespoons chopped fresh thyme and/or flat-leaf (Italian) parsley

The key to selecting wines for long-simmered stews is to match the generous character of the dish without overpowering it. Adequate levels of tannin are required to counterbalance the richness of the marbled meat. The cinnamon, allspice, and cloves are background flavors that many big red wines possess.

DEPENDABLE: CABERNET SAUVIGNON–BASED BLEND FROM FRANCE
DARING: LIGHTLY AGED NEBBIOLO FROM NORTHWESTERN ITALY

SERVES 4

❀ To make the marinade, combine the garlic, parsley, thyme, orange zest, peppercorns, cloves, allspice, and cinnamon stick on a square of cheesecloth (muslin). Bring the corners together and tie securely with kitchen string. Pour the wine and ¼ cup (2 fl oz/60 ml) olive oil into a deep non-aluminum container and add the onions and cheesecloth bag.

❀ Add the beef to the marinade, stir, cover, and refrigerate for 24 hours.

❀ Preheat an oven to 300°F (150°C).

❀ Remove the meat from the marinade and pat dry. Reserve the marinade. In a heavy sauté pan over high heat, warm 2 tablespoons of the olive oil. Brown half of the meat on all sides, 5–10 minutes. Transfer the browned meat to a heavy pot. Add the remaining 2 tablespoons oil to the pan and brown the remaining meat. Add it to the pot. Add the reserved marinade, including the cheesecloth bag, and the tomatoes. Add water as needed just to cover. Cover, bring to a boil over high heat, transfer to the oven, and bake until meltingly tender, 3–4 hours.

❀ While the beef is cooking, bring a saucepan three-fourths full of salted water to a boil. Add the carrots and cook until tender when pierced with a knife, about 10 minutes. Drain and set aside.

❀ When the beef is tender, remove from the oven and discard the cheesecloth bag. Using a large spoon, skim off the excess fat from the surface. Add the carrots and olives and place over medium heat until heated through. Season with salt and pepper.

❀ Transfer to a warmed serving bowl or serve directly from the pot. Sprinkle with the chopped thyme and/or parsley just before serving.

NUTRITIONAL ANALYSIS PER SERVING: Calories 699 (Kilojoules 2,936); Protein 46 g; Carbohydrates 26 g; Total Fat 47 g; Saturated Fat 10 g; Cholesterol 142 mg; Sodium 432 mg; Dietary Fiber 6 g

Chocolate Decadence Cake

PREP TIME: 15 MINUTES

COOKING TIME: 15 MINUTES,
    PLUS 3 HOURS FOR
    COOLING

INGREDIENTS

1 lb (500 g) semisweet chocolate,
broken into small pieces

1 cup (8 oz/250 g) unsalted butter, at
room temperature, cut into pieces

¼ cup (2 oz/60 g) granulated sugar

1 tablespoon all-purpose (plain) flour

4 eggs, separated

1 package (12 oz/375 g) unsweetened
frozen raspberries, thawed

1 cup (8 fl oz/250 ml) heavy (double)
cream

2 tablespoons confectioners' (icing)
sugar

1 teaspoon vanilla extract (essence)

½ pint (4 oz/125 g) fresh raspberries
(optional)

Chocolate desserts like this one are challenging partners for most wines because they are both bitter and sweet. Dry Cabernet Sauvignons work well when the chocolate is more bitter than sweet, but here you need a sweeter wine.

DEPENDABLE: RUBY OR VINTAGE PORT
DARING: ORANGE MUSCAT

SERVES 6

❈ Preheat an oven to 425°F (220°C). Butter an 8-inch (20-cm) springform pan, line with parchment (baking) paper, and butter the parchment.

❈ Place the chocolate in a heatproof bowl or the top pan of a double boiler. Set over (not touching) gently simmering water in a saucepan. Stir gently until melted. Remove from the heat and whisk in the butter, granulated sugar, and flour. In another bowl, lightly beat the egg yolks until blended. Add to the chocolate mixture and whisk to blend.

❈ In yet another bowl, using an electric mixer, beat the egg whites until they hold their shape but are not stiff. Using a rubber spatula, fold them into the chocolate mixture. Spoon into the prepared pan.

❈ Bake for about 15 minutes. The cake will still be wiggly. Leave in the turned-off oven to cool for 1 hour with the oven door ajar. Then, to set the cake, place in a freezer for at least 2 hours (or refrigerate for up to 8 hours). Release the pan sides and unmold onto a plate. Discard the parchment. Thaw and bring to room temperature before serving.

❈ Meanwhile, place the thawed raspberries in a blender and purée until smooth. Pour through a fine-mesh sieve to remove the seeds. Cover and refrigerate, then bring to room temperature before serving.

❈ In a bowl, using an electric mixer or a whisk, beat together the cream and confectioners' sugar until soft peaks form. Using a rubber spatula, fold in the vanilla. Cover and refrigerate until serving.

❈ Dipping a sharp knife in hot water before each cut, slice the cake into narrow wedges and transfer to individual plates. Drizzle with the raspberry sauce and top with the whipped cream. Sprinkle each serving with a few fresh raspberries, if desired.

NUTRITIONAL ANALYSIS PER SERVING: Calories 910 (Kilojoules 3,818); Protein 9 g; Carbohydrates 70 g; Total Fat 73 g; Saturated Fat 44 g; Cholesterol 281 mg; Sodium 76 mg; Dietary Fiber 4 g

Caramelized Walnut Tart

PREP TIME: 35 MINUTES,
    PLUS 2 HOURS FOR CHILL-
    ING AND FREEZING PASTRY

COOKING TIME: 1½ HOURS

INGREDIENTS

FOR THE PASTRY

1½ cups (7½ oz/235 g) all-purpose (plain) flour

2 tablespoons brown sugar

pinch of salt

½ cup (4 oz/125 g) chilled unsalted butter, cut into slivers

1–2 tablespoons ice water, or as needed

FOR THE FILLING

1¼ cups (10 oz/315 g) granulated sugar

½ cup (4 fl oz/125 ml) water

3 cups (12 oz/375 g) chopped walnuts

¾ cup (6 oz/185 g) unsalted butter, at room temperature, cut into slivers

1 cup (8 fl oz/250 ml) heavy (double) cream

⅓ cup (3 oz/90 g) honey

Several classic fortified wines, including tawny port and cream sherry, echo the aromas and tastes in this sweet, rich tart of caramel and nuts. A sweet Madeira works best to cast a lemony, refreshing complexity over the dessert.

DEPENDABLE: SWEET MADEIRA BASED ON BUAL OR MALMSEY
DARING: TAWNY PORT

SERVES 8

❈ To make the pastry, in a food processor, combine the flour, brown sugar, and salt and pulse to combine. Add the butter and process until the mixture resembles cornmeal. Add about 1 tablespoon ice water and mix until the dough just holds together, adding more ice water if the mixture is too dry. Gather into a ball, place in plastic wrap, and refrigerate for at least 1 hour or for up to 2 days.

❈ On a lightly floured work surface, roll out the dough into a round ¼ inch (6 mm) thick. Transfer to a 9½- or 10-inch (24- or 25-cm) tart pan with a removable bottom. Trim the pastry even with the pan rim. Cover and place in a freezer for 1 hour. Refrigerate the trimmings.

❈ Preheat an oven to 400°F (200°C). Line the pastry shell with aluminum foil and fill with pie weights. Bake until slightly set, 10–15 minutes. Remove from the oven and remove the weights and foil. Patch any holes with the reserved pastry trimmings. Reduce the oven temperature to 375°F (190°C).

❈ To make the filling, in a saucepan over high heat, combine the granulated sugar and water and bring to a boil, stirring until the sugar dissolves. Boil rapidly until the mixture thickens and changes color, 10–15 minutes. When pale brown, remove from the heat and stir in the nuts and butter and then the cream. Return to low heat and simmer until very thick, 15–20 minutes. Stir in the honey, remove from the heat, and let cool slightly.

❈ Line a baking sheet with aluminum foil. Pour the filling into the pastry shell and place on the baking sheet to catch any spills. Bake until lightly browned, 25–35 minutes. Let cool completely on a rack.

❈ Remove the pan sides and slide the tart off the pan bottom onto a serving plate. Cut into wedges to serve.

NUTRITIONAL ANALYSIS PER SERVING: Calories 922 (Kilojoules 3,872); Protein 11 g; Carbohydrates 77 g; Total Fat 67 g; Saturated Fat 27 g; Cholesterol 145 mg; Sodium 47 mg; Dietary Fiber 3 g

Peach or Nectarine Gratin

PREP TIME: 15 MINUTES

COOKING TIME: 8 MINUTES

INGREDIENTS

4 cups (1½ lb/750 g) peeled, pitted, and sliced ripe peaches or nectarines, at room temperature

1½ teaspoons lemon juice

½ teaspoon almond extract (essence)

1 cup (8 oz/250 g) sour cream

2 tablespoons milk or half-and-half (half cream)

¼ cup (2 oz/60 g) granulated sugar

½ cup (3½ oz/105 g) firmly packed brown sugar, or as needed

MAKE-AHEAD TIP: Several hours before serving, you may assemble the fruit in a baking dish, then refrigerate it along with the sour cream topping.

Orchard fruits, such as peaches, apricots, and nectarines, call for wines with similarly fruity and floral character, especially when the fruits are at their peak of ripeness. Late-harvest Rieslings, with peach and nectarine flavors, are naturals, as are oak-aged Sauternes-styled wines, which highlight the nuttiness of the almond extract.

DEPENDABLE: LATE-HARVEST RIESLING
DARING: DEMI-SEC SPARKLING WINE

SERVES 4

❁ Preheat a broiler (griller).

❁ Butter a flameproof 9-inch (23-cm) square baking dish. Place the fruit on the bottom of the prepared dish. Sprinkle with the lemon juice and ¼ teaspoon of the almond extract and toss lightly.

❁ In a bowl, whisk together the sour cream, milk or half-and-half, the remaining ¼ teaspoon almond extract, and the granulated sugar. Spoon the mixture evenly over the fruit. Sprinkle the ½ cup (3½ oz/105 g) brown sugar evenly over the sour cream layer, adding more brown sugar if needed to cover.

❁ Slip the dish under the broiler 4–5 inches (10–13 cm) from the heat source and broil (grill) until the brown sugar melts, 6–8 minutes. Remove from the oven and serve at once.

NUTRITIONAL ANALYSIS PER SERVING: Calories 358 (Kilojoules 1,504); Protein 3 g; Carbohydrates 60 g; Total Fat 13 g; Saturated Fat 8 g; Cholesterol 29 mg; Sodium 54 mg; Dietary Fiber 3 g

Berry Crisp

PREP TIME: 30 MINUTES

COOKING TIME: 40 MINUTES

INGREDIENTS

FOR THE FILLING

⅔ cup (5 oz/155 g) granulated sugar

¼ cup (1½ oz/45 g) all-purpose
(plain) flour

pinch of salt

1 tablespoon grated orange zest

1 tablespoon kirsch (optional)

1 teaspoon vanilla extract (essence)

6 cups (1½ lb/750 g) assorted
berries such as blueberries, black-
berries, raspberries, and boysen-
berries, in any combination

FOR THE STREUSEL TOPPING

¾ cup (4 oz/125 g) almonds or
hazelnuts (filberts)

1½ cups (7½ oz/235 g) all-purpose
(plain) flour

½ cup (3½ oz/105 g) firmly packed
brown sugar

½ cup (4 oz/125 g) granulated sugar

1 teaspoon ground cinnamon

½ teaspoon ground ginger

pinch of salt

½ cup (4 oz/125 g) chilled unsalted
butter, cut into small pieces

1 cup (8 fl oz/250 ml) heavy (double)
cream

There is a natural berry and plum characteristic in ruby and vintage ports, which pairs magically with this dessert. The younger
and simpler the wine, the better it resonates with the ginger
and cinnamon in the topping. If you like, serve the crisp with
whipped cream in place of the pouring cream. About 3 pounds
(1.5 kg) prune plums, pitted and sliced or quartered, can be
used in place of the berries.

DEPENDABLE: RUBY OR VINTAGE PORT
DARING: CALIFORNIAN BLACK MUSCAT

SERVES 4

❈ Preheat an oven to 350°F (180°C). Butter a 10-inch (25-cm) oval or
rectangular baking dish.

❈ To make the filling, in a small bowl, stir together the granulated
sugar, flour, salt, orange zest, the kirsch (if using), and the vanilla. Place
the berries in another bowl, scatter the sugar mixture over the top, and
toss gently to mix. Pour into the prepared baking dish.

❈ To make the topping, spread the nuts on a baking sheet and toast in
the oven until they take on color and are fragrant, 5–8 minutes. Remove
from the oven, let cool, and chop. Raise the oven temperature to 375°F
(190°C).

❈ In a bowl, stir together the nuts, flour, brown sugar, granulated
sugar, cinnamon, ginger, and salt. Add the butter and, using a pastry
blender or 2 knives, cut in until the mixture resembles coarse cornmeal.
(Alternatively, process the flour mixture briefly in a food processor until
mixed, then add the butter and pulse until the mixture resembles coarse
cornmeal.) Pat the mixture evenly over the fruit.

❈ Bake until the top is golden and bubbles appear at the sides of the
dish, 25–30 minutes. Transfer to a rack.

❈ Serve the crisp warm. Pass the cream in a pitcher at the table.

NUTRITIONAL ANALYSIS PER SERVING: Calories 1,202 (Kilojoules 4,292); Protein 15 g;
Carbohydrates 153 g; Total Fat 63 g; Saturated Fat 30 g; Cholesterol 147 mg; Sodium 128 mg;
Dietary Fiber 11 g

Coffee Pôts de Crème

PREP TIME: 15 MINUTES

COOKING TIME: 35 MINUTES,
   PLUS 2 HOURS FOR
   CHILLING

INGREDIENTS

1½ cups (12 fl oz/375 ml) heavy
   (double) cream

½ cup (4 oz/125 g) sugar

3 tablespoons instant coffee (or
   espresso) powder

¾ teaspoon vanilla extract (essence)

4 egg yolks

MAKE-AHEAD TIP: These intense
custard creams can be made up to
2 days before you plan to serve them.

A custard's silky texture makes it one of the best desserts to highlight after-dinner wines. The essential coffee flavor present here blends gracefully with nut and toffee nuances, so serve tawny ports, sweet (India Brown) sherry, or Bual-based Madeira.

DEPENDABLE: TAWNY PORT, PREFERABLY OLDER THAN 10 YEARS
DARING: BEAUMES-DE-VENISE (MUSCAT FROM FRANCE)

SERVES 4

❈ Preheat an oven to 325°F (165°C).

❈ Pour the cream into a saucepan and place over medium heat until small bubbles appear along the edges of the pan. Add the sugar, instant coffee, and vanilla and stir until the sugar and coffee dissolve. Remove from the heat.

❈ In a bowl, whisk the egg yolks until blended. Slowly add the hot cream mixture while whisking constantly to prevent curdling. Pour through a fine-mesh sieve into four 1-cup (8–fl oz/250-ml) custard cups or ramekins. Place the containers in a baking pan and add hot water to reach halfway up the sides of the containers. Cover the pan with aluminum foil.

❈ Bake until just set but the centers still move slightly when the containers are shaken, about 35 minutes. Remove from the oven and carefully remove the cups from the water bath. Let cool until you can touch a cup, then cover them all with plastic wrap. Chill for at least 2 hours before serving.

NUTRITIONAL ANALYSIS PER SERVING: Calories 484 (Kilojoules 2,033); Protein 5 g; Carbohydrates 32 g; Total Fat 38 g; Saturated Fat 22 g; Cholesterol 335 mg; Sodium 42 mg; Dietary Fiber 0 g

Custardy Bread Pudding

PREP TIME: 20 MINUTES, PLUS
  1 HOUR FOR STEEPING

COOKING TIME: 40 MINUTES

INGREDIENTS

2 cups (16 fl oz/500 ml) half-and-half
  (half cream)

1 cup (8 fl oz/250 ml) heavy (double)
  cream

½ cup (4 oz/125 g) granulated sugar

2 orange zest strips, each about
  2 inches (5 cm) long

6 slices fine-textured white bread,
  crusts removed and cut on the
  diagonal into triangles

4–5 tablespoons (2–2½ oz/60–75 g)
  unsalted butter, at room
  temperature

4 whole eggs, plus 2 egg yolks

1 tablespoon vanilla extract (essence)

¼ cup (1 oz/30 g) confectioners'
  (icing) sugar

1 cup (4 oz/125 g) sliced strawberries
  or whole raspberries or blueberries

The silky texture of bread pudding, like those of custard-based desserts, mimics several sweet wines. A late-harvest Chenin Blanc works particularly well because of its acidity, which can cut the dessert's richness. The bread contributes a toasty flavor, which opens the door for an oak-aged wine. If desired, serve the pudding with a pitcher of heavy cream in place of the berries.

DEPENDABLE: LATE-HARVEST CHENIN BLANC
DARING: AUSTRALIAN LATE-HARVEST MUSCAT

SERVES 6

❋ In a saucepan, combine the half-and-half, heavy cream, granulated sugar, and orange zest. Place over high heat and bring to a boil, stirring to dissolve the sugar. Remove from the heat and let steep for 1 hour. Pour through a fine-mesh sieve placed over a clean saucepan.

❋ Preheat an oven to 350°F (180°C).

❋ Spread the top side of the bread triangles with the butter. Arrange them, overlapping, on the bottom of a 2-qt (2-l) baking dish.

❋ Return the cream mixture to medium heat until small bubbles appear along the edges of the pan. Remove from the heat. In a bowl, whisk together the whole eggs and egg yolks until blended. Slowly add the hot cream mixture while whisking constantly to prevent curdling. Whisk in the vanilla. Holding the sieve over the bread-lined baking dish, strain the cream-egg mixture into the dish to immerse the bread. Place the baking dish in a baking pan. Pour hot water into the pan to reach halfway up the sides of the dish.

❋ Bake until the top is golden brown and just set, but the center still moves slightly when the dish is shaken, 30–40 minutes. Transfer to a rack and, using a sieve, dust the top with the confectioners' sugar. Let cool to lukewarm or room temperature.

❋ Scoop servings onto individual plates and scatter some of the berries over each portion.

NUTRITIONAL ANALYSIS PER SERVING: Calories 559 (Kilojoules 2,348); Protein 11 g; Carbohydrates 43 g; Total Fat 39 g; Saturated Fat 22 g; Cholesterol 320 mg; Sodium 231 mg; Dietary Fiber 1 g

Warm Gingerbread

PREP TIME: 20 MINUTES

COOKING TIME: 40 MINUTES,
   PLUS 15–20 MINUTES FOR
   COOLING

INGREDIENTS

3 cups (15 oz/470 g) all-purpose
   (plain) flour

2 teaspoons baking powder

1½ teaspoons ground cinnamon

1 teaspoon ground ginger

½ teaspoon salt

¼ teaspoon ground cloves

¼ teaspoon ground pepper

1½ teaspoons baking soda
   (bicarbonate of soda)

1½ cups (12 fl oz/375 ml) boiling
   water

1 cup (11 oz/345 g) dark molasses

½ cup (4 oz/125 g) unsalted butter,
   at room temperature

1 cup (7 oz/220 g) firmly packed
   brown sugar

2 eggs, lightly beaten

3 tablespoons peeled and grated
   fresh ginger

1 tablespoon grated lemon zest

1½ cups (12 fl oz/375 ml) heavy
   (double) cream

¼ cup (1 oz/30 g) confectioners'
   (icing) sugar

The fragrant personality of gingerbread—at once sweet, spicy, and piquant—requires precise wine choices. Italian dessert wines, especially Vin Santo (which has many of the same flavors), are an epiphany with this dessert.

DEPENDABLE: VIN SANTO OR OTHER ITALIAN DESSERT WINE
DARING: HUNGARIAN TOKAY

SERVES 8

❋ Preheat an oven to 350°F (180°C). Butter and flour a 9-by-13-inch (23-by-33-cm) baking pan. Tap out the excess flour.

❋ In a bowl, sift together the flour, baking powder, cinnamon, ground ginger, salt, cloves, and pepper.

❋ In another bowl, dissolve the baking soda in the boiling water. Stir in the molasses and set aside to cool.

❋ In a stand mixer fitted with the paddle attachment, combine the butter and brown sugar and beat on medium speed until light and fluffy. Slowly add the eggs, beating constantly. Beat in the fresh ginger and lemon zest. Using a rubber spatula, scrape down the sides of the bowl. Reduce the speed to low and gradually add the flour mixture alternately with the molasses mixture, stopping to scrape down the sides of the bowl often. The batter will be very thin. Pour into the prepared pan.

❋ Bake until a toothpick inserted into the center of the gingerbread comes out clean, 30–40 minutes. If the gingerbread is browning too quickly, cover loosely with aluminum foil. Transfer to a rack and let cool until warm.

❋ Just before serving, in a bowl, using an electric mixer or a whisk, whip together the cream and confectioners' sugar until stiff peaks form.

❋ Cut the gingerbread into squares and place on individual plates. Top each serving with a dollop of the whipped cream.

NUTRITIONAL ANALYSIS PER SERVING: Calories 683 (Kilojoules 2,867); Protein 8 g; Carbohydrates 96 g; Total Fat 31 g; Saturated Fat 18 g; Cholesterol 147 mg; Sodium 570 mg; Dietary Fiber 2 g

GLOSSARY

You'll find the following list of common wine terms and their definitions a useful reference when reading this book's introductory pages and the wine recommendations that accompany the recipes, as well as when you read about, shop for, or order wines.

ACIDITY

The tart element of a wine's flavor, resulting from more than half a dozen different natural fruit acids, chief among which are tartaric, malic, and citric acids. Acidity is a key factor to consider in matching a wine with food, because it has the ability to contrast with rich ingredients or sauces, to marry well with tart foods, or, more generally, to refresh or cleanse the palate. Wines with too little acidity taste dull; those with too much, unpleasantly sharp.

APERITIF

Applies in general to a wide range of wines and spirits that are offered before a meal, on their own or accompanied with hors d'oeuvres to stimulate the appetite. Among the most popular aperitif wines are sherry, Madeira, and Champagne and other sparkling wines. More and more, however, light white wines such as Sauvignon Blanc and lighter types of Chardonnay are also enjoyed as aperitifs.

APPELLATION

Most often seen with reference to French wines and paired with the word *Contrôlée* or *d'Origine Contrôlée*. Both terms appear on the labels of French varietal wines. The former guarantees that the wine was produced in the region indicated in the name, while the latter guarantees both the place of origin and a certain level of quality. More generally, it refers to the region in which any wine was made.

AROMA

The distinctive fragrance of a particular varietal wine, described in terms of the grape variety or varieties from which it was made and other flavors developed during the wine-making process, including those reminiscent of other fruits, herbs, or spices. Most often, the term applies only to the scent of relatively young wines, before they develop a more complex bouquet.

ASTRINGENCY

The sensation of sharpness or bitterness a wine causes in the mouth and on the tongue. A certain level of astringency can provide a pleasing, palate-cleansing contrast to rich foods. Very astringent wines, resulting from a high level of acidity or too much tannin, will cause the mouth to pucker or will feel harsh or rough on the tongue or the back of the throat.

BALANCE

A wine described as "well balanced" will present harmonious levels of fruit, acidity, tannin, oak, alcohol, and sugar, each making its presence felt without dominating or concealing the others.

BARREL-AGED

When a wine is matured in oak barrels after its initial fermentation, its alcohol leaches from the wood certain chemical compounds that contribute to its overall flavor and aroma, as well as help stabilize it. Barrel-aging is most often used for more complex white and red wines.

BODY

The sensation of substance a wine produces in the mouth, often described in terms of weight, fullness, or texture. Among the many elements of a wine's structure that contribute to its body are its levels of alcohol and tannin, as well as the presence of glycerin, which develops during the fermentation process, and of compounds leached from the oak barrels in which it is aged. Sweet dessert wines also gain an impression of full body from the higher levels of sugar they contain.

BOUQUET

Although related to aroma, this term more specifically describes the rich, complex, heady fragrances that are smelled and appreciated in a mature wine as the result of the aging process it undergoes while in the barrel and the bottle.

BREATHING

A wine breathes when it comes in contact with the air by being opened and poured into glasses at table or transferred to a decanter a few hours before serving. Some wines benefit from breathing. The bouquet of well-aged bottles, for example, may develop more fully, although they should not be opened so far in advance that some of their qualities may be lost. Harsh young wines high in acidity and tannin can sometimes gain some smoothness through the breathing process. Typically, red wines benefit more from breathing than white wines do.

CARAFE

The term for a classic stopperless bistro-style glass container, distinguished by a simple hour-glasslike, widemouthed form that lends itself to easy grasping and pouring. In France, these are regularly used for serving modest house wines, commonly drawn directly

from a barrel and offered by the whole or smaller half carafe. A carafe may also be used as a decanter.

CHAMPAGNE

Although the term *Champagne* is often erroneously used to describe any sparkling wine, true Champagne refers only to the sparkling wines from the northern French region of the same name. These are produced from Pinot Noir, Pinot Meunier, and Chardonnay grapes in strict accordance with the centuries-old *méthode champenoise,* by which the wine undergoes a secondary fermentation in the bottle, resulting in its distinctive bubbles of carbon-dioxide gas.

COMPLEXITY

Refers to a wine that offers a multidimensional experience, with many different fine, well-balanced elements to be appreciated in its bouquet and flavor.

CORKED

Quality wines are sealed in their bottles with corks cut from the bark of cork oak trees, and the possibility exists—estimated by some experts to be as high as 1 in 20—that any individual cork may prove to be defective, causing the wine to become spoiled, or corked. Corked wines develop an off flavor that at its mildest is perceived as flatness and at its worst resembles moldy cardboard.

CUVÉE

Derived from the French *cuve,* or "vat," this term refers to the result of blending together different batches of wines to achieve a desired end product that is then bottled. In the making of Champagne, the *cuvée* is a vineyard's proprietary blend of still wines that then undergoes the secondary fermentation.

DECANTER

A special container, often with matching stopper, into which wines may be transferred, or "decanted," from their original bottles before being served. The decanting process is most often used to promote the breathing of fine older wines, which are poured from their original bottles very slowly and carefully so that none of the sediment that might be found on the bottom of the bottle transfers to the decanter. Although a simple carafe may be used as a decanter, more often these are specially made containers of handblown or cut glass befitting the quality of the wines they are destined to hold.

DRY

Refers to a wine in which little or no trace of sweetness may be detected. Wines with just a hint of sweetness are described as off-dry. Those slightly sweeter, but still appropriate for serving with savory foods are termed medium-dry.

ESTATE-BOTTLED

Used and accepted on a wine label in the English language as a designation of quality, this describes a wine that has been made entirely at the winery from grapes grown on lands that the winery itself owns or controls. Similar terms exist in other languages, chief among which are the French *mis en bouteilles, mise à la propriété,* or *mis en bouteilles au château;* the Italian *imbottigliato all'origine;* and the German *Gutsabfüllung* and *Erzeugerabfüllung.*

FERMENTATION

Caused by yeasts, this natural chemical process converts grape sugars into alcohol and carbon dioxide, thereby turning grape juice into wine. As the level of alcohol in the liquid rises to about 14 percent, the yeast dies off, ending fermentation.

FINISH

The tastes and textures that remain in the mouth after a sip of wine has been swallowed. Wines with pleasant finishes that linger (sometimes referred to as "long" finishes) are often considered better than those with little or no finish.

FLAVOR

The simple or complex impression of tastes a wine presents, which may be described in terms of the grape or grapes from which it was produced; the oak barrels in which it was aged; and any other impressions it may convey, including those that embrace other fruits or vegetables, herbs or spices, chocolate, and other distinctive tastes.

FRESH

Usually describes the light, clean taste of rosé, white, and some younger red wines, often marked by a pleasant edge of acidity and a fruity aroma.

FRUITY

Usually describes the flavor or aroma of a young, fresh wine that presents impressions not only of the grapes from which it was made, but also of other fruit such as apples, berries, peaches, or tropical fruits.

LATE-HARVEST

A designation for wines made from grapes that were deliberately left on the vine for picking late in the harvest, causing the fruits to shrivel and develop higher levels of sugar. As a result, late-harvest wines are usually sweet and are served after a meal, either on their own or with complementary desserts.

MADEIRA

A fortified wine originating on, or made in the style of, the Portuguese island of Madeira. Stored for at least 3 months in a warm room or tank, and then sometimes further aged in wooden casks, the wine gradually develops a distinctive flavor reminiscent of burnt caramel. The alcohol levels of Madeiras are fortified to as high as 20 percent, and they vary from mellow and nutty-tasting dry varieties, which may be offered as an aperitif, to sweet, robust Madeiras commonly served after dinner. When other wines have been overly aged and stored under excessive heat, they may develop an oxidized flavor and tawny hue described as "Madeirized."

OAK

The wood of choice for making the barrels or casks in which fine wines are usually aged. Oak imparts its own distinctive flavor and bouquet, along with its own tannins, to wines. The term is also used to describe that particular element of a wine's flavor or bouquet.

PORT

Sweet and full bodied, this Portuguese fortified dessert wine is traditionally made in and around the city of Oporto. Those designated

tawny have been aged in wood for 5 years or more, developing a mellow flavor and tawny hue.

RESERVE

No standard or legal definitions exist for this term, which is sometimes found on wine labels. It is most often used, however, as a marketing strategy to designate a bottling of wine specially produced by a particular vineyard from grapes of a higher quality and handled with extra care by the winemaker.

SEDIMENT

As quality wines, particularly reds, age, various compounds, including tannins, pigments, fruit acids, and tartrates, gradually separate from the liquid as fine granular deposits known as sediment, visible if the bottle is held up to a light source. While sediment is harmless, it can mar the full appreciation of a wine if it finds its way into the glass. For this reason, bottles containing sediment should be allowed to rest upright for a day or so to allow all particles to settle to the bottom; then, before serving, they should be opened, disturbing the contents as little as possible, and slowly poured into a decanter. The decanting ends when the first traces of sediment become visible in the bottle's neck.

SHERRY

Its name an Anglicization of Jerez, the southern Spanish town in and around which it is traditionally produced, this fortified wine ranges in alcohol level from 17 to 22 percent. Three basic types of sherry exist: *fino,* which develops a pale straw color and tangy flavor from a particular strain of yeast that protects the wine from oxidizing as it ages in partially filled oak barrels; *amontillado,* which is nuttier and fuller-bodied than *fino;* and *oloroso,* which is more pungent than the other two, taking on a distinctive flavor reminiscent of nuts and dried fruit as it oxidizes in the barrel. Most good-quality sherries are naturally dry, although some may be sweetened to make so-called cream sherries.

SPARKLING WINE

Refers to any wine that includes tiny bubbles of carbon-dioxide gas suspended in the liquid. Most classically, these are produced by the *méthode champenoise* developed to make the fabled Champagne of France, by which the wine undergoes a second fermentation inside its bottle through the introduction of yeast cells and sugar. Other sparkling wines, generally of lesser quality, may be fermented a second time in large pressurized tanks, a  process known as Charmat, bulk, or *cuve close.* The least expensive of sparkling wines gain their fizz through the artificial introduction of gas.

TANNINS

These organic compounds are present in varying degrees in the stems, skins, and seeds of grapes, especially those used to make full-bodied red wines, as well as in oak aging barrels. Tannins give wine its astringency and edge of bitter flavor, as well as helping to preserve it during the aging process. The higher the level of tannins in a wine, the more likely it is to age well.

TASTE

A general wine-tasting term meant to embrace the overall flavor sensations of a particular wine.

VINTAGE

This term refers specifically to the year in which particular grapes for a wine were harvested. By extension, it refers to any wine made and ultimately bottled from grapes harvested in a specific year and therefore reflecting the quality of that harvest and the skills and artistry of the particular vineyard and its winemakers.

VARIETALS

Predominantly in the Americas, Australia, South Africa, and New Zealand, wines made entirely or mostly from a single variety of grape are known as varietal wines, a departure from the European tradition of naming a wine after the region in which it is produced. Those varietals most commonly found in wineshops and referred to in this book are:

CABERNET SAUVIGNON

Made from a robust grape variety noted for such qualities as its fruity, spicy, or herbaceous flavor and high level of tannins, this varietal is considered among the best of red wines. The same grape yields the great red wines of France's Médoc and Graves regions in Bordeaux.

CHARDONNAY

One of the most popular of varietals produced in the United States, Australia, and South Africa, this is a dry, fruity, rich, and complex white wine. Chardonnay grapes are also the source of France's great white Burgundy wines such as Chablis, Côte de Beaune, Mâcon, Meursault, and Montrachet. They are also among the grapes commonly used in the *cuvées* of Champagne.

GEWÜRZTRAMINER

Made from a grape variety originating in northern Italy, Alsace, and Germany and now also grown in America, Australia, and New Zealand, this white wine is noted for a flavor that is distinctively spiced (*gewürtz* in German), as well as rich, soft, and fruity, and that ranges from fairly dry to somewhat sweet.

MERLOT

A red varietal appreciated for its fruity flavor and rich, full body, Merlot is the predominant grape in a few great French wines of Bordeaux's Saint-Émilion and Pomerol districts.

PINOT NOIR

Considered by many to be the greatest red wine grape of France, source of the great wines of the Burgundy region, Pinot Noir is noted for its complexity, distinguished by abundant, rich flavor and bouquet described in terms of fruit, spice, and flowers, and coupled with a body sometimes described as silken.

RIESLING

Made in its native Germany and elsewhere, this great white varietal is appreciated for its floral bouquet, crisp acidity, and a complexity of flavor that brings comparisons to fresh peaches and apricots, flinty minerals, and even smoke. Rieslings range from crisp and dry to sweet after-dinner, late-harvest varieties.

SAUVIGNON BLANC

This fresh, fruity varietal is often described in terms of its grassy, herbaceous flavors and crisp acidity and is usually best appreciated in its youth. The Sauvignon Blanc grape is also a key element of the great white Bordeaux wines of France, from Sauternes to Graves. It is also found in the eastern part of the Loire Valley.

ZINFANDEL

A red wine grape of California that traces its ancestry back to southern Italy, Zinfandel produces several basic types of varietal wines: white Zinfandels, crisp whites noted for their fresh, fruity flavor and blush of pink color; light young reds reminiscent of France's Beaujolais nouveau; strong, hearty reds high in tannins and with flavors recalling berries, cherries, and spice; and sweet late-harvest Zinfandels.

INDEX

ACKNOWLEDGMENTS

The publishers would like to thank the following people and associations for their generous support and assistance in producing this book:
Desne Border, Ken DellaPenta, Kathryn Meehan, Vivian Ross, and Hill Nutrition Associates.

The following kindly lent props for photography: Fillamento, Williams-Sonoma, and Mark Harrington Glassware of San Francisco, CA; and Bale Mill Country Furniture, St. Helena, CA. Some of the wines used in this book were provided by Kermit Lynch of Berkeley, CA; and Paul Marcus Wines of Oakland, CA. The photographer would like to thank Plump Jack Winery in Oakville, CA, for generously sharing their lovely grounds for location photography. He would also like to thank Chromeworks and ProCamera, San Francisco, CA; and FUJI film for their generous support of this project. Special acknowledgment goes to Daniel Yearwood for the beautiful backgrounds and surface treatments.